L. M. MONTGOMERY:

AN ASSESSMENT

Edited by

JOHN   ROBERT   SORFLEET

CANADIAN CHILDREN'S PRESS GUELPH

The articles contained herein were published in part in *Canadian Children's Literature*, No.3 (1975).

Canadian Children's Press
Box 335
Guelph, Ontario N1H 6K5

ISBN# 0-920512-00-3

Printed in Canada

Table of Contents

Introduction

Articles

L. M. Montgomery: Canadian Authoress

Were Lucy Maud Montgomery alive today, she would be one hundred years old. She could look back on a very productive life: twenty-three books of fiction, one book of poetry, a book about courageous women, and an autobiography. Her works have been read and enjoyed by millions, both children and adults. The fiction still sells steadily in countries as diverse as Canada and Japan. In fact, Anne Shirley is probably Canada's best-known fictional export.

It is in recognition of L. M. Montgomery's work that this collection of articles has been assembled. It seems especially appropriate that the cover art for the collection is a reproduction of the Canada Post Office's own tribute to Montgomery's centennial: Peter Swann's portrait of Anne. He has depicted Anne as we first meet her, sitting on a pile of shingles while waiting with carpetbag for Matthew at the railroad station. The "faded brown sailor hat" is missing, and the "very short, very tight, very ugly dress of yellowish-gray wincey" is somewhat altered, but the red hair and large eyes are very much Anne's. Though Swann's conception may not be perfectly coincident with another reader's "mind's-eye" portrait, he has made a commendable attempt to reproduce in art the Anne he has seen in his imagination.

The body of this collection is comprised of seven articles. Elizabeth Waterston, in the initial article, presents a survey of Montgomery's life and work. She indicates the early childhood influences and the later adult career of L.M.M., as well as providing informative and perceptive comments on all the books.

The following pair of articles focuses on the Anne books. Mary Rubio discusses Montgomery's attitude to satire, realism, and imagination through careful comparison of *Anne of Green Gables* with Mark Twain's *Tom Sawyer* and *Huckleberry Finn*. Putting Montgomery's novel in the context of then-contemporary literature, Rubio reveals its particular quality and achievement. Gillian Thomas, in contrast, looks at the later Anne books. She suggests reasons for their apparent decline from the level of the first novel.

Anne Cowan moves away from Anne and chooses to centre her comments primarily on the Emily trilogy, especially in regard to Emily's authorial talents--talents shared, of course, by Emily's creator. By considering both Emily Byrd Starr and L.M.M. as *Canadian* authoresses, she adds to our understanding of the intrinsically Canadian nature of Montgomery's work.

Muriel Whitaker, taking a different approach, deals with a variety of novels: the first Anne, Emily, and Pat books plus *The Blue Castle*. Her concern is with Montgomery's heroines, with what makes them--especially Anne and Emily--such memorable characters. Jane Fredeman's article also examines the heroines of various novels, but she puts the emphasis on the fantasy worlds that they create. She sees the conflict between fantasy and reality as a major tension in all the books, and she indicates how the situation is resolved in specific instances. Incidentally, like Cowan and Whitaker, she gives some emphasis to the Emily series in the course of her discussion.

The final article, appropriately, is by another well-known children's writer, Jean Little, whose books, like Montgomery's, have sold thousands and thousands of copies. Little divides Montgomery's children into four types: Stock Children, Non-Children, Exaggerated Children, and Real Children. In the last group her favourite is Jane of Lantern Hill because, unlike Anne and Emily who are *exceptional* real children, Jane is a comparatively *ordinary* real child.

The seven articles provide good coverage of the range of Montgomery's fiction. However, since only Elizabeth Waterston's survey mentions the non-novelistic *Watchman and Other Poems* (1916) and *Courageous Women* (1934), perhaps a few additional words on these books are in order. The former is a collection of previously published poems; some are interesting, but none are exceptional. Curiously enough, one of the poems is titled "At the Long Sault"--a title and topic Archibald Lampman had also used shortly before his death in 1899, though the poem was not published until 1943. There is, therefore, no question of influence one way or the other; in any case, Montgomery's treatment is much less dynamic and much more conventional than Lampman's. Still, *both* were sufficiently interested in that incident from Canada's past to make it the subject of poetry.

Courageous Women, which Montgomery wrote in collaboration with Marian Keith and Mabel McKinley, shares this concern with Canada's past. Though the twenty-one biographies include such world-renowned figures as Joan of Arc and Helen Keller, a full fifteen--over 70%--are about Canadian women: Madeleine de Vercheres, Laura Secord, Catherine Parr Traill, Ada May Courtice, Caroline MacDonald, Elizabeth Louise Mair, Anna Gaudin, Sadie Stringer, Madame Albani, Pauline Johnson, Aletta Elise Marty, Dr. Margaret Mackellar, Margaret Polson Murray, Lady Tilley, and Marshall Saunders. All made notable contributions to Canada and/or humanity in spite of many obstacles,

5

thus the appellation, "courageous". The book is valuable because it clearly affirms both Montgomery's Canadianism and her feminism. As she wrote as early as 1909 in a letter to Ephraim Weber,

> But I *do* believe that a woman with property of her own should have a voice in making the laws. Am I not as intelligent and capable of voting for my country's good as the Frenchman who chops my wood for me, and who may be able to tell his right hand from his left, but cannot read and write?

> So you wish 'married women everywhere were real companions to their husbands'. So do I--as heartily as I wish that married men everywhere were real companions for their wives. You can't, as Emerson says, cut this matter off with only one side. It has to have two. As for 'spheres', I believe anyone's sphere--whether man or woman--is where they can be happiest and do the best work. The majority of women are happiest and best placed at home, just as the majority of men are in the world. But there are exceptions to both. Some women are born for a public career, just as some men are *born* to *cook in a restaurant*. Yes, they are! And each has a right to fulfil the purpose of their birth. Sex seems to me to enter very little into the question. There is no sex in mind, I do believe, and--'let each one find his own', and her own, in business as well as matrimony.

During the last few years, new information about Montgomery and new stories from her hand have come to light. The source of the material is a trunkful of diaries, manuscripts, and other papers now owned by Montgomery's surviving son, Dr. Stuart MacDonald of Toronto. The diaries provided the basis for a recent CBC television special on Montgomery and revealed the inner passionate woman behind the outward conventional mask. The stories, originally assembled as an unpublished MS titled "The Blythes Are Quoted", have been reorganized and published as *The Road to Yesterday* (McGraw-Hill Ryerson, 1974). In spite of what one or two reviewers have contended, the volume contains some quite pleasant stories. There is, perhaps understandably, a little too much reference to the Blythe family as a standard of comparison, and a few of the stories tax credibility. However, as a whole, the stories are reasonably enjoyable--even humourous--and are quite consonant with Montgomery's other fiction. They also contain certain realistic events not commonly considered to be part of Montgomery's fictional world. In "A Commonplace Woman", for example, the protagonist--who has quite enthusiastically engaged in a secret love affair without any thought of marriage, who gives birth to an illegitimate child then surrenders her for adoption by a wealthy couple, and who later secretly murders her daughter's husband because he cruelly mistreats his wife and child--is allowed to live to the ripe old age of 85 and is quite content on her deathbed. Indeed, when she dies, her eyes are "triumphant and young", and her last words assert "I have lived!"--an evaluation with which Montgomery seems to concur. This is a far cry from the Sunday school fiction of Montgomery's early career.

Taken together, the articles in this collection provide a fitting commemorative tribute to L.M. Montgomery and to the child, woman, and author that she was. However, the best tribute is probably that which each of us gives in our repeated reading of the fiction. Anne, Emily, Marigold, Valancy, Pat, Jane and all the others--we prove--are alive . . . and living in Canadians.

JOHN R. SORFLEET

Articles

Lucy Maud Montgomery
1874-1942

ELIZABETH WATERSTON

She was born on a beautiful island. Her mother died when she was very young. Her father left her with an old lady and an old man, in an apple-orchard, by the sea. When she grew up, she was put under a vow, never to leave the old people. But a young man loved her, and after ten years of waiting he carried her off, away from the island. [1]

This is the language of fairy-tale. It seems to be the first way to tell the story of Lucy Maud Montgomery. Girls following her biography in H. M. Ridley's *Life of L. M. Montgomery* may feel they are reading another romance in the sequence of "Anne" and "Emily" and "Pat" and "Story Girl" books.

Many women *have* lived "fabulous" lives. But in L. M. Montgomery's case the real miracle is that she could exploit her experience in an enduring art-form. She universalized her story; she recreated it against vivid regional settings; she structured it into mythical patterns. She retold the legends she had lived, in haunting and memorable style.

She used her life materials in a way that brought her personal fame, and brought her country's literature a popular international recognition. Literary critics throughout the Western world saw at once the values she had achieved. If subsequent sophisticated criticism agreed to laugh at or to by-pass the creator of ''Anne,'' critics today are less ready to be patronizing.

We find in her life, her letters, her journals, the story of an important craftsman, a professional writer fighting to clarify and improve the conditions of an artist's work. And in her novels we find a subtle and illuminating use of archetypal patterns, particularly of the recurring myths of girlhood.

If we re-examine her life story and look at her books as in part an unconscious supplement to the biography, we come close to watching the miracle of the creative imagination.

Born in 1874, in a North Shore village on Prince Edward Island, Lucy Maud Montgomery was brought as a baby from Clifton to

Cavendish, to her mother's family. Her grandmother MacNeill gave her a home when her young mother, Clara Woolner MacNeill Montgomery, died twenty-one months after Lucy Maud's birth. Her father, Hugh John Montgomery, left the Island to strike out for the West, and settled in Prince Albert.

Lucy Maud Montgomery's memories of childhood were very intense. She could recall "spots of time" from her third year on. She was a bright, quick child: when she started school she moved eagerly through the old P.E.I. "readers," with their characteristic Maritime blend of New England and British writers. Years later she would place on the title-pages of her books verses from the same range of great Romantic and Victorian writers of America and Britain: Whittier, Emerson, Longfellow, Oliver Wendell Holmes; and Tennyson, Byron, Cowper, and Burns.

Life was dominated by the grandparents' notions of how a little girl should dress and behave. She was a solitary child, creating imaginary friends, and living in the book-worlds of Bunyan and Scott and Thackeray. Slowly and sensitively she realized the beauty of her native setting: the apple-orchard slopes of the MacNeill farm; the red-earth, tree-lined road winding past pond and woods to the village of Cavendish; the blueberry barrens; and the circling, sounding sea.

She responded, and she wrote. She phrased her impressions of the world around her in the formal and already old-fashioned diction of Thomson's *Seasons*. She liked, later, to tell the story of showing her earliest lines to her family--who complained, "It doesn't rhyme!" But one point of the story is that although she defended the "blankness" of her verse, she was willing to re-work it, producing soon reams of rhyme. It was a first, characteristic effort to adjust to critical suggestions. From the beginning it was not just self-expression that she wanted--it was recognition. She wanted to write, but she also wanted to be read. She sent off her first manuscript, hopefully, when she was eleven, to an American magazine, *The Household*. It was returned, but she tried again, this time for a Canadian publication. It would be four years before her first appearance in print, but those years were characterized by an amazing persistence. Composing, copying, mailing, continued in the face of total lack of interest--this would not be in the scope of most twelve-year-old, thirteen-year-old, fourteen-year-old lives.

The first heartening acceptance came for a verse-narrative, reworking a P.E.I. legend, sent to the Charlottetown *Patriot*. This was in the winter of 1889-90, and the manuscript was sent from the far West, for Lucy Maud had now moved out to Prince Albert to join her father. From Prince Albert, while she was in high school, she sent other poems and sketches to Montreal, to Charlottetown, and to New York.

The reunion with her father was brief. He had remarried and although she enjoyed the company of her step-brother and step-sisters, the adolescent girl did not fit comfortably into the new home. The year, so productive of immediate literary work, never seemed "usable" later: she by-passed it when she was expoiting other events of her girlhood and assigning bits of her own experience to her fictional heroines.

Meanwhile, the young Islander trailed back to Cavendish to finish school and to write entrance examinations for Prince of Wales College. In 1893 she moved to Charlottetown to attend the College (where courses covered the final two years of high school and the first two of university). Her one-year course qualified her for a teacher's licence. In the same year she had her first "pay" for literary work: two subscriptions to the magazine that accepted her poem, "Only a Violet." It was an American magazine.

L. M. Montgomery (as she now signed her manuscripts) continued to write and submit stories and poems to Canadian and American magazines, after she had taken her teacher's licence and begun to work at Bideford School. Most of the manuscripts came back, but enough were accepted (though without any monetary reward) to make the young author decide to get further training in the field of literature. She went to Halifax in 1895, enrolled at Dalhousie College, and took a course in English literature from Archibald MacMechan, himself a poet and short story writer. The alternative for an Islander would be McGill--many of the characters in her stories go to the Montreal university; but L. M. Montgomery's formal education was all in the Maritimes. During her year in Halifax she earned her first money for writings: five dollars from *Golden Days* in Philadelphia; five dollars from the *Halifax Evening Mail;* twelve dollars from the Philadelphia *Youth's Companion.* She was also placing more and more work with the Sunday School papers, enough to encourage her ambition for a career as a writer.

In 1896, back on Prince Edward Island, school-teaching left little time or energy for composition. But for many months she worked at her writing each morning from six to seven, by lamplight, sitting on her feet to keep warm in the old farmhouse where she was boarding.

She resigned her teaching job two years later to return to Cavendish. The death of her grandfather MacNeill in 1898 left her grandmother alone. L. M. Montgomery decided to see if she could make a living by her writing, eked out by the money her grandmother made as local postmistress. Lucy Maud was twenty-two years old; she was selling enough to cover board and clothing; she was improving her work. "I never expect to be famous," she wrote. "I merely want to have a recognized place among good workers in my chosen profession." In the year after her grandfather's death, in double dedication to family and career, she promised her grandmother to stay and work at home.

Briefly, she interrupted her Island life when she accepted a job on the Halifax *Daily Echo* in November, 1901. She moved into a Halifax boarding-house, and for almost a year wrote a weekly gossip column, edited a page of society letters, proof-read, answered the phone, and did free "write-ups" of the advertisers' goods. She was learning to work under pressure, to produce for a given audience. Meantime she could submit manuscripts to other publications, with a growing percentage of acceptances. She was sending to more sophisticated journals now: *Ainslie's, The Delineator, The Smart Set,* published in the eastern States.

11

The young author acquired "pen-pals" among other young people aspiring to literary success. She began an interesting correspondence, for instance, with Ephraim Weber, a Kitchener man who had gone homesteading in Alberta, but shared her literary ambitions and frustrations: "We'll be dead long before Canadian literature will be a bread-and-butter affair." By June, 1902, she was writing all her friends to tell them she was going home to the Island, hoping for more free time for writing.

Settled again in Cavendish, she was beginning a long courtship with a young Presbyterian minister, the Reverend Ewan Macdonald, a fine-looking man a few years older than she, and product of the same kind of schooling and family. She worked hard at her sketches and stories, mailing them to a great variety of magazines: *Canadian Magazine, McClure's,* the *Family Herald, Current Literature,* the Boston *National, Sunday School Times,* the Battle Creek *Pilgrim, Modern Women,* New York *Gunton's, Lippincott's.* Her letters are filled with indefatigable zest and eager interest in the possibilities for publication. She was reading *Trilby, Dr. Jekyll and Mr. Hyde, The Story of an African Farm,* the poetry of Markham, catching up on contemporary best-sellers. She was puzzling over matters of faith, the possibility of psychic experience, the mystery of pain, evolution, the divinity of Christ, eagerly discussing, exploring, opening her mind to any new trend of thought. She was simultaneously re-exploring the Bible, Gibbon's *Decline and Fall of the Roman Empire,* and Emerson. The best way to catch a notion of her work at this time is to read *Further Chronicles of Avonlea,* published much later, but consisting mostly of stories written in her early twenties, *"pot-boilers"* as she herself scornfully dubbed them, but intriguing in their range of interests.

She could report making $591.85 in 1904. Ideas for stories and poems came fast, caught into notebook jottings, set aside till a mood or a market suggested a way of "working up." She could pass along practical advice: *"To work at once, stick to it,* write something *every day,* even if you burn it up after writing it."

In 1904, she re-read a note-book entry: "Elderly couple apply to orphan asylum for a boy. By a mistake a girl is sent them." Although her first intention was to work this notion into a short story for a Sunday School paper, she found the character "grew on her" so much that the work expanded to book length. She worked on it for eighteen months, keeping other writing on the go at the same time. The manuscript was mailed out hopefully to a publisher, and rejected. Mailed again, three more times, to other possible publishers, including Macmillan. Rejected again--and finally stowed away by the author in discouragement.

Meanwhile she had placed another story, *Kilmeny of the Orchard,* in serial form, with an American magazine, and other stories with the Chicago *Blue Book,* New York *Watson's,* Chicago *Rural Magazine.* She made about $800 in 1906, but by dint of unremitting writing. She rarely left Cavendish; her grandmother was now eighty-two, and the younger woman had almost all the housework to do. She was reading less, and an odd mixture : the Book of Job, Upton Sinclair's "hideous" *The Jungle,* Lewis Carroll's *Alice through the Looking Glass.*

Then spring came, and wonderful news. The manuscript of *Anne of Green Gables,* which she had dug out, re-worked, and sent off to one more publisher, was accepted. "I am blatantly pleased and proud and happy," she said, "and I shan't make any pretence of not being so."

The L. C. Page Company of Boston, "her" publisher, was not a major house, but they did handle Bliss Carman, Charles G. D. Roberts, and other writers well known to Maritime readers. They offered 10 percent royalties (nine cents on a wholesale price of ninety cents), plus a flat sum for dramatic rights, and bound her to give them first refusal of all her books for the next five years. Pitman's of London would hold the English rights. On the whole, acceptable terms, and certainly a glorious realization of the long, long dream of having a full-length book published.

In June, 1908, the first copy of *Anne of Green Gables* arrived from the publishers, attractively bound, in good clear print on good firm paper—a format that would stand up to the readings and re-readings that awaited it when it reached the hundreds of thousands of its young audience.

The book instantly appealed to an incredibly large market, and one not limited to girls. It brought floods of letters to its author, including a note from Bliss Carman, and one from Mark Twain. The proud author thrilled to Mark Twain's comment: in Anne she had created "the dearest, and most lovable child in fiction since the immortal Alice." *Anne of Green Gables* went into four editions in three months, and rolled on from there into one printing after another.

The terms of the publishers' contract did not include any sliding scale of royalities for this run-away best-seller. If the author wanted to cash in on the "Anne-mania" she must get to work on a sequel. The publishers insisted that she should write "like mad" to meet the demand. She settled into a new routine: two hours of writing, one of transcribing onto the typewriter—thinking out plot and dialogue as she worked around the house. She was less than happy with her new book. It didn't "grow"; she had to "build" it. She blocked it all out in her mind before writing it. "All the incidents have happened...and I have only to write about then now."

Meanwhile she house-cleaned, sewed, gardened, played the organ for the church choir. The Reverend Ewan Macdonald was still hovering near, trying to persuade her to marry him. He found adamant refusal for a number of reasons: her grandmother, her writing commitments, her career, her new book—reasonable barriers multiplied. There were still serious puzzles in her religious thinking also: "I call myself a Christian, but oh!"

In November, 1908, she sent off the manuscript of *Anne of Avonlea.* She was feeling tired, head-achey, nervous, worn out by the publicity surrounding "that detestable Anne." "Petty flings of malice and spite" followed local readings of the book. She was brooding over "certain worries and troubles that have seemed ever present in my life for the past six years [i.e., since 1902]. They are caused by people and circumstances over which I have no control, so I am quite helpless in regard to them and when I get rundown I take a too-morbid view of them." A favourite aunt died in 1909. That year she refused an invitation to speak at a World's Congress of Women in Toronto: "couldn't get away."

But in the fall of 1909 she started a new book—beginning by composing the first sentence and the last paragraph. *The Story Girl* she considered "away ahead of *Anne* from a literary point of view." She enjoyed writing this tale of a golden summer, a gathering on the Island of a family group, focused and dramatized by the story-telling skill of the one gifted cousin. Writing this nostalgic book about the "few opulent months" gave the author great pleasure. It occupied her most of 1910. While it was in the making her publishers brought out *Kilmeny of the Orchard (1910)*, a re-working of a story previously published serially.

The Story Girl was published in May, 1911. The year had already brought a major change in L. M. Montgomery's life. Her grandmother died, at the age of eighty-seven, thirteen years after the grandfather's death and the restraining promise to stay on. Lucy Maud Montgomery now felt free to marry, in July, 1911, Ewan Macdonald, and to set out on a wedding trip to England and Scotland. Like the teen-age trip to her father in Prince Albert, this long voyage never seemed usable to the author. There are no references in any of her later books to the sights and experiences of this long-dreamt-of tour. She returned to Canada, not to Prince Edward Island, but to Leaskdale, Ontario, where Mr. Macdonald had accepted a call.

When she left the Island, L. M. Montgomery had produced four works of unequal value. *Kilmeny of the Orchard* is fervid in style, melodramatic in plot. It followed a contemporary fad for books about psychosomatic impairment. Kilmeny's dumbness is not unlike the hysterical crippling of the child in *The Secret Garden* (1911), and her pathos is linked with that of "Freckles" in Gene Stratton Porter's novel (1904), her violin-playing with that of *The Girl of the Limberlost* (1912). *Trilby* contributes something to the tone. But L. M. Montgomery set her plot of impediment released by love in an Island setting. Kilmeny in her magic trance is guarded by an old aunt and uncle and a gypsy boy, in the best Gothic tradition, but her Eden is a clearly realized orchard, with "real toads"—and an indoor world of antimacassars.

In *Anne of Green Gables*, the world of dour propriety is assaulted by the daemonic force of a red-headed child brought miraculously from "off the island." This book seems almost untouched by timely fashions in "girls' stories." It opens its casements into timeless myths of youth and growth and the quest for identity. Every incident in it is at the same time vivid and deeply suggestive: Anne comes down a long lane with Matthew, to the old farm where angular Marilla sits between a west window flooded by sunlight and an east window framing a cherry tree in bloom but "greened over by a tangle of vines." Anne dyes her red hair green. She is given first a brown dress by Matthew, then a green one by Marilla. Anne makes her "kindred spirit," Diana, drunk, just before she herself walks a ridge-pole and breaks an ankle. Midway through the book she breaks a slate over Gilbert's head, then must work out her resentment of him and accept his "friendship" as the book ends. Psychologists today would interpret the story symbolically; they would suggest that reading such a story probably helps young girls accept imaginatively the processes of growing up and edging toward adult physical passion. For the millions of girls who have "identified" with Anne, these deep patterns *may* work in some such subconscious way; but the book satisfies also in its romantic pantheism, its regional humour, and its fresh sense of the excitement of language. L. M. Montgomery knew more than the psychologists about the dreams and the anxieties of adolescent girls; her childhood loneliness, her early power of expression and her suspended maturing had kept open the channel to "lost time."

A glance at *Anne of Avonlea* shows a decrease of power. Anne, "half-past sixteen," putting in a year of teaching, is a "Sleeping Beauty." All action rises from minor characters. They interest because they represent types that will recur: a cranky old man from New Brunswick; a pair of ill-matched twins; a gifted, poetic "Yankee" boy; a long-waiting spinster. L. M. Montgomery was not yet ready for a real study of late adolescence. Anne's romance builds no suspense. (There are good regional bits still, such as Mrs. Lynde's view of a neighbour: "a slack-twisted creature who washes her dishes sitting down.")

The Story Girl might seem at first reading equally episodic. But the book begins on a May morning on the road to an orchard-farm, and runs rhythmically to November, when "the sharp tops of the spruces" stand "Against the silvery sky." It presents three mysteries: that of the old "witch," Peg Bowen; that of the secret chamber of the "Awkward Man", and that of the family "blue chest," heritage of broken romance. The "Story-Girl," Sara, motherless, gifted, differs from Anne in that her father exists though in the background. (Anne, we remember, dreamt of being called "Cordelia," like Lear's loving daughter.) And Sara's circle can meet with the grown-up world of adults, occasionally, but happily, at twilight, in the orchard. The boy who tells the story knows himself to be only temporarily on "the Island." The identification of island with orchard with spring with youth is tactfully handled and effective. All these things give organic unity to *The Story Girl*. They justify L. M. Montgomery's own fondness for the book.

She had now left Cavendish and the routines of her old home. The new life would have its new routines: running the manse, helping with parish work, women's groups, choirs, Sunday school. New duties would be added, a year later, with motherhood. Like most women-writers of her generation she had always had at least two lives: that of producing artist and that of conscientious house-keeper. The "woman's world" was hers by no choice of her own. What woman in 1912, in a small provincial town, could expect to resign from this sphere? The artist's world was a different matter. There was nothing automatic in the intense

15

determination that freed a couple of hours a day for writing and revising, and kept the imagination active in undeviating devotion to a régime of steady craftsmanship. L. M. Montgomery had inherited some special talent, and had grown up in a gossipy community where anecdotes were valued, and a good raconteur much admired; she had worked at her craft in hope of money and a career. But now the real mystery appears: what force, what drive, what aspirations powered the undeviating drive on through the long string of successful books, one every other year, from the year of her marriage till 3 years before her death? Not only for the royalty money, welcome as that was in a small-town manse, but for other rewards, she found time to detach herself from the "real" world of Leaskdale, to continue the tales of the other "reality," she remembered island of adolescence.

Chronicles of Avonlea was published in 1912. In this set of Island stories Anne Shirley appears very briefly, and rarely as a moving force. These tales of proud poverty, of loneliness, of frustrated courtships are interesting experiments in point of view. Romance and sensibility are filtered through the practical viewpoint of matter-of-fact narrators, the unpoetic neighbours who watch poignant events. "Sentiment and humour" (as L. M. Montgomery says of one of the *Chronicles* characters) "wage an equal contest."

The Golden Road (1913) is an elegy on childhood. It completes the seasonal cycle of *The Story Girl*, running from December through the riches of summer to "sere" autumn in the orchard setting. Most mysteries of the earlier book find rather prosaic fulfilment: a bride for the Awkward Man, a visit to church for the Witch. The "Story-Girl," Sara, tells a new cycle of tales: Indian and classical legends, and local folk tales, while her sad alternate, Sara Ray, suffers new repressions. The children's rituals and fears are convincing and funny. But the family disperses as the book ends, and a sadness tinges the story.

Perhaps the elegiac mood reflected the author's entry into a new phase of life. Her first son, Chester Cameron, was born in 1912. A second infant, Hugh, born in 1914, lived only for a day. In 1915 the birth of Ewan Stuart completed the Macdonalds' family.

By this time, war had broken out, and the manse was touched by the tension in all Canadian life. L. M. Montgomery turned once again to the story of Anne, to satisfy "all the girls all over the world who [had] wanted more." It was a relief to escape to girlhood and romance and the friendships and escapades of student days, "pre-war."

Anne of the Island (1915) takes Anne away to the mainland and to maturity. Anne is at college, involved in the love-stories of her friends and in a delusive romance with "Royal Gardner." Gilbert lurks near, offering apples. Anne rejects his first offer of love, in a very real moment of tension and fear. The reconciliation at the close is autumnal and subdued. The whole book is perfectly adapted to its audience of adolescent girls, in its timidity, its repressions, and its lyric romanticism and idealism. The book is "real" too in the gentle growth of Anne's friendships with other girls as she comes nearer to a sense of her own identity. The moving climax to this development occurs when a "Mainland" friend takes her to "Bolingbroke," her birthplace, where she feels "not an orphan any longer."

The major weakness in plot is the ending, when Anne's "spell" is broken, and she accepts her love for Gilbert, because of a melodramatic sudden illness and miraculous cure. But such a resolution is acceptable in myth; and once again L. M. Montgomery had released mythic energies in the story she had created. She had prepared for such a supervenience of miracle by the recurring use of symbolic settings, suggestive of Eden. The tone of the closing is wistful, perfect for its insecure audience and its saddened time.

Emotions stirred by the war had led L. M. Montgomery to a revived activity in poetry. In 1916 she brought out *The Watchman and Other Poems,* dedicated to the Canadian soldiers who had died in the war. The title poem is a meditative monologue on the first Easter, in a manner reminiscent of Browning. The other poems, lyrics of sea, of hills and woods (rather heavily fraught with dryads and dingles and fisher-folk and moonrise) are mostly reprints from a surprisingly long list of magazines, *Youth's Companion, Forward, Maclean's Magazine, East and West* — and fifteen others, all markets for occasional poems. These are Edwardian, water-colour descriptions:

> Elusive shadows linger shyly here
> And wood-flowers blow, like pale, sweet spirit-bloom,
> And white, slim birches whisper, mirrored clear
> In the pool's lucent gloom.

This volume marks an important change. It was published by the Canadian firm of McClelland, Goodchild and Stewart in 1916, and by Stokes of New York in 1917. Constable's of London issued an English edition in 1920. The old connection with the Page Company of Boston was broken. The galling sense that she had had less than a fair return for the best-selling *Anne of Green Gables* had irked L. M. Montgomery throughout the five-year period when she was bound to give Page's the first refusal of her new books. Now she moved happily into an arrangement that involved a reputable Canadian publisher along with American and British affiliates. (English rights were later transferred from Constable's to Hodder and Stoughton.)

In the next six years, the new publishers brought out *Anne's House of Dreams (1917), Rainbow Valley (1919),* and *Rilla of Ingleside (1921).* All three are shadowed by war. The focus moves from Anne to her Family. Even in *Anne's House of Dreams* Anne and Gilbert have become unreal, and their friends seem phoney and sentimental. Owen Ford speaking:

> "The rose is the flower of love — the world has acclaimed it so for centuries. The pink roses are love hopeful and

17

> expectant — the white roses are love dead and forsaken — but the red roses — ah, Leslie, what are the red roses?"
> "Love Triumphant," said Leslie in a low voice.

Not low enough, say we — but the author seems unable to suppress this false strain. The real vitality in the book lies in the middle-aged, gossipy ladies, Susan and Miss Cornelia.

The gossip continues in *Rainbow Valley*, easing the shadow of world catastrophe into the small talk of neighbours and pets. Anne's young family are joined by the motherless brood at the nearby manse. Her own children are shadowy, and she herself is reduced to some cliché gestures ("hands clasped before her") and "tag" descriptions (shining grey eyes"). A newcomer joins the range of types: Mary Vance, an orphan, but a brassy, skinny, pale-eyed, pugnacious one. The widowed minister, dreamily abstracted from his children's needs, is firmly realized also. And how L. M. Montgomery must have enjoyed "naming" the children of this Presbyterian minister: Jeremy and Carlyle, turbulent Faith and gentle Una!

The play of names in *Rilla of Ingleside* is thought-provoking too. It is Walter, named after Anne's father, who is killed — the father dies again, in a sense. Marilla's namesake adopts a war-baby, Jims, while Jem, given up as dead, lives again at the end. Nan and Di, the twins, are "off-stage" most of the time although the notion of twins still seems to press on L. M. Montgomery's fancy.

The book makes an interesting contrast with *Anne of the Island*. Anne's daughter waits through a four-year period for her romance, just as the mother had done, but the inhibition is imposed from without, by war. In a little experiment with first-person point-of-view, Rilla recounts her waiting in her journal — a preview of the major method of the Emily Books which will come soon.

These three "Anne" books were brought out by the new publisher in a format similar to the earlier volumes. Their sales were excellent.

Trouble flared in 1920 when the former publisher, Page's of Boston, brought out a collection of early pieces, which had appeared years before as magazine sketches, under the title *Further Chronicles of Avonlea*. Their reasoning seems to have been that the author had owed them "refusal" on these stories. L. M. Montgomery indignantly protested against "piracy," and decided to sue for invasion of her rights. The suit dragged on for about nine years, wearying, sometimes embarrassing and humiliating, always irritating and distracting. This battle over the publishers' "right" to the book was important for professional writers. It stirred furious discussion in authors' associations, and spot-lighted the need for business acumen and a readiness to fight for due rewards. It revived all the old tensions over copyright and piracy which which had so long plagued Canadian writers.

Of the book itself, L. M. Montgomery spoke slightingly. But there are at least two aspects worth notice. First, a number of ghost stories in the late Kipling manner reflect the author's interest in psychic phenomena and her ability to blend new ideas about extra-sensory perceptions with the old patterns of folk tale. Second, the "Western" sketch, "Tannis of the Flats," set in Prince Albert, and reminiscent of Bret Harte and Owen Wister, catches attention as a single use of that alien setting experienced briefly when Lucy Maud Montgomery visited her father in the 1880s.

The furore about her lawsuit increased her status among Canadian writers. She was in demand as a speaker at literary societies, and was still bombarded with letters and questions about her methods of working and the "originals" of Anne and of Green Gables.

In 1921 she had the rather unhappy experience of seeing a silent movie based on her book but distorting many elements in it. Her old contract with the Page Company gave her no royalties for "screen rights," and she had no control over the revision of the story for movie purposes. She particularly objected to the school-room scenes, in which the Stars and Stripes flew bravely over the P.E.I. school-house.

Perhaps the tension over rights to the products of her imagination, combined with this public focus on its processes, led L. M. Montgomery to a new subject. She went back again to the memory of her own girlhood, and began the story of a girl living between the world of fact and the world of words. "Emily" is a character whose joy and release consist of writing—first a letter journal to her dead father, then a set of sketches in her "Jimmy-books" (note-books offered by a sympathetic old cousin) and finally tales and poems, proffered to publishers.

The theme of a writer's ambition had been a sub-current in early "Anne" books. Now it becomes a major strand. In the three "Emily" books (*Emily of New Moon, Emily Climbs,* and *Emily's Quest*), chapters of Emily's journals reflect and intensify the third-person narrative sequence.

Emily of New Moon (1923) is an intriguing book even without this looking-glass effect. In it L. M. Montgomery moves powerfully into a mythical tale of girlhood. Names of people and places half-reveal and half-disguise the undercurrents of meaning and emotion. The little girl named Emily Byrd Starr comes from Maywood to the New Moon farm of her mother's people (the mother was named Juliet). Her false friend is Rhoda (rodent?), her true friend is Ilse (ipse?). Her first teacher is Miss Brownell (who destroys imagination), her second Mr. Carpenter (who, obviously, builds). Midway through the book a priest encourages her to "keep on" writing; but at Wyther Grange she meets a man *named* Priest—Dean Priest at that—the crippled "Jarback," her own dead father's friend, who brings her to life again, at the cost of possessing her soul. None of this is obtrusive, but it adds a dimension of interest to the surface story. That story is an intriguing though unpretentious version of Wordsworth's *Prelude,* a careful recreation of those "spots of time" in which the creative imagination is nurtured. It clarifies the directions of a growing child's fantasy-life. The story is climaxed by a mysterious vision in which Emily's mind, in delirium, fuses three bits of memory, and prophetically "sees" a hidden truth (the "real" story of Ilse's lost mother). This prophetic second sight restores Ilse to her estranged father, by clearing the dead mother's reputation. It is an effective fable of art. It is also a good solution of the double plot, a fusion of Emily's "real" life among her friends and her life as poetic creator.

Having opened the doors of memory so far, L. M. Montgomery pushed them wider—perilously wider—in her sequel. *Emily Climbs* (1925) recreates the tone of a teen-aged girl's view of life: her sense of being misunderstood and repressed, her obsessive interest in her own identity. Emily had gone to "Shrewsbury," to the town where shrewish Aunt Ruth waits to curb, censor and belittle her. Yet in spite of never being understood Emily manages to enjoy, innocently, most forbidden pleasures. This fantasy of adolescence is a precursor of *Catcher in the Rye, A Separate Peace* and the whole fashionable swarm of such books. It expresses the romance and dreaminess of adolescence, as well as the arrogance, self-pity and inhibitions we have been taught ruefully to recognize. The material is awkwardly handled: the structure and style seem to have some of the clumsiness and unsureness of the adolescent. But the book is a pioneering entry into a difficult and important area.

It is no accident that L. M. Montgomery's first mature attempt at an adult novel came as an interruption of the "Emily" series. *The Blue Castle (1926)* was an effort to "climb" past the stereotypes of girls' books.

In 1925 the permanence of her appeal was marked by the beginning of a re-issue of her work in a "uniform edition" (Harrap, 1925-1935). Her family life had made a welcome shift, from Leaskdale in the rather remote Uxbridge area, to the larger town of Norval, near Toronto, and in the centre of the earlier settled regions of western central Ontario. Here Mr. Macdonald hoped for an easing of his duties, since his health was not good. The Macdonalds' sons were now boys of thirteen and ten. Perhaps the vigorous reality of their lives suggested a vivid alternative to the retrospective dreams of remembered childhood.

The Blue Castle is energetic and tough. It is an amazingly blunt story of a frustrated woman's attempt to find a real life in defiance of family tabus and conventions. It has a Cinderella plot, but the settings and characters mark a definite break from cliché. The story begins with a pompous family dinner party, which may echo Galsworthy but which certainly precedes *Jalna (1927)*. It moves to "the verge of up-back," to the derelict home of a drunken no-good, and from there to a roaring barn-dance brawl at Chidley's Corners. Exactly half-way through, Valancy (what a nice name for an independent Canadian heroine!) accepts joyfully the fact of her love for the mystery man from Muskoka, and moves with him to an enchanted island. In the second half of the book the author piles up improbable plot twists with jaunty unconcern, without losing the sardonic realism of her portraits of the family group left behind in "civilization." Valancy's Dionysian revolt is blurred a little by the third plot thread—her devotion to the romantic nature-writings of "John Foster." But as one young reader says, "you can skip the John Foster stuff," and keep a book with real vitality: a fairy-tale set to a jazz tempo.

The reviewers were not impressed. Professor Desmond Pacey some years later summarized the contemporary reaction: "all the weaknesses of the Anne books and none of their redeeming charm." L. M. Montgomery had an over-developed sensitivity to reviews. She had an old habit of quoting reams of critical comments to her friends, to her correspondents, to lecture audiences. Good or bad, she found reviews very important. In *The Blue Castle,* reviewers had missed the special quality she was aiming for, or had not found it impressive.

In 1927, *Emily's Quest* marked the author's retreat from her experimental venture. This is another "girls' book," in magazine style. The familiar characters are re-assembled, re-aligned, and finally sorted out into romantic pairs. "Jarback Priest,"after threatening to become a distinct person, diminishes and fades as conventional poetic romance takes over. The book makes an interesting pair with *The Blue Castle,* so different in tone.

In 1929 another gifted fantasy-child was added to the established pattern, in *Magic for Marigold.*

Then came one more attempt to break the mold. *A Tangled Web* (*1931*) is an effort at mosaic method in plotting a story for grown-ups. *Aunt Becky Began It* was the English title of this novel—Aunt Becky being the old-witch character who dangles a family treasure before the Dark-Penhallow clan and sets its members to weaving a number of webs in hope of the heirloom. This folk-tale motif of treasure and hag-guardian has recurred in almost every one of L. M. Montgomery's novels. The novel "up-dates" the Island girls, now lipsticked, silkstockinged, bobbed, and given to small swearings. The author offers a cheap "come-on" in the opening paragraph when she implies that we will learn how Big Sam Dark "learned to appreciate the beauty of the unclothed female form." But in spite of this minor naughtiness the stories are still the conventional tales of "Avonlea,"not really lifted into any newly mature vision.

The author had now an impressive list of still-popular books to her credit. A new generation was"growing up on Anne," and the production of new books had settled to a rhythm of one novel every alternate year. A new movie version of *Anne of Green Gables* was in the making (to be released in 1934). A number of tours of Canada, east (every summer) and west, had shown the author how universally popular her books continued to be, and how strong the demand for"more about the Island."

During these years at Norval she added two more to her list of seventeen books: *Pat of Siver Bush* (*1933*) and *Mistress Pat* (*1935*). "Pat" is a convincing child in her deep attachment to her home and her dread of change and chance. "Old Judy Plum," the Irish housekeeper who watches the child's initiation into maturity, becomes wearisome in her stage-Irish mannerisms, but she delighted (and still delights) young readers. Dialect humour holds its appeal for children.

L. M. Montgomery's own "children" were now young men ready for university. Perhaps the give-and-take of their boyhood life together was now far enough distanced in the author's memory to have become accessible for re-creation. Such a theory of the way her imagination worked, at a distance in time from experienced fact, might account for the new strength in the "Pat" books of studies of family life. Brother-and -sister relations, not well handled or handled with false sentimentality in *Rainbow Valley* and *Rilla of Ingleside*, are better managed now, with new variety and a sometimes rueful realism.

Before leaving Norval, L. M. Montgomery found time also to collaborate on a compilation of lives of *Courageous Women (1934)*. The list of women includes Pauline Johnson, Marshall Saunders, Madame Albani, and Catharine Parr Traill, along with non-Canadian "heroines" such as Joan of Arc, Florence Nightingale and Helen Keller. The collaborators were Mabel Burns McKinley and Marian Keith (Mrs. Donald MacGregor). Mrs. MacGregor had been a treasured friend since 1911, the year both young women, newly established authors and newly married brides of ministers, had met at a Toronto reception given by the Women's Press Club. It was a friendship that perhaps exerted unfortunate pressures on L. M. Montgomery to conform to the conventions of romantic escapist fiction of the moral uplift sort.

The Macdonald family moved to Toronto in 1935 when Mr. Macdonald retired from the active ministry. Life centred around the activities of the two university students, Chester in law and Stuart in medicine. The Women's Press Club, the Canadian Author's Association, and other groups of professional and amateur artists absorbed time and energy. So did the business of arrangements with publishers, and the still voluminous correspondence with friends, relations and readers. She was herself an omnivorous reader of classics, mystery stories, best sellers, magazines — anything and everything.

In this year of flattering official recognition, 1935, L. M. Montgomery appeared on the King's Silver Jubilee List as an officer in the Order of the British Empire. She was also elected Fellow of the Royal Society of Arts and Letters. The Institut des Lettres et des Arts of France made her a member, and later awarded her a silver medal for literary style.

She set to work again in her new home on Riverside Drive in Toronto, to rebuild the pattern of plotting, writing, and revising, all dove-tailed into the daily chores of housekeeping. Two last "Anne" books were to be written: *Anne of Windy Poplars (1936)* and *Anne of Ingleside (1939)*. These stories are concocted to "fill in the gaps" in Anne's story: the years spent in waiting for Gilbert to finish his medical course (*Windy Poplars*) and the years when her children were small (*Ingleside*). Both books have a warmed-over flavour. The people are "characters" revived from earlier models. Neither book has distinction in structure. The slang is an odd mixture of phrases of the 1930s and the remembered cadences of the 1900-1910 period. Even "Susan" has lost her gossipy vigour. Anne's children are quaint and cute and not very believable.

22

But there remained one further flame of creativity. One last girl would be added to the roll-call of convincing heroines. *Jane of Lantern Hill (1937)* begins in Toronto. It is a Toronto of dreary grey mansions and more dismal filling-stations, family dinners, and ashy back-yards. But Jane goes every summer from this Toronto to join her father on Prince Edward Island. Eventually she draws her golden mother with her, back to the Island. This small and poignant version of Orpheus and Eurydice ends in pastoral reunion and fulfilment. It is equally vivid in its Island paradise, where Jane keeps house for her father, and in its Toronto hell, where Jane quakes before Grandmother (who calls her "Victoria"). If, as Professor Northrop Frye says, literature is "two dreams, a wish-fulfilment dream and an anxiety dream, that are focussed together, like a pair of glasses, and become a fully conscious vision," this last book stakes a claim as literature. Not just "children's literature," either, for both Jane's anxiety and her dream are successful metaphors of adult psychic realities. Jane's island paradise is deeply meaningful and satisfying; and not only for children.

L. M. Montgomery was increasingly conscious of her role as mythmaker. She talked mystically about "the Island" as a place of the soul. Asked to contribute an article on P.E.I. to a memorial volume on Canada, designed for presentation by the Canadian Pacific Railway to King George and Queen Elizabeth, L. M. Montgomery sidestepped the expected conventions of travel-book descriptions. She wrote of the Island's beauty, its reality, its peace; the feeling it gave, in "dimming landscape...and long, white-sand beach and murmuring ocean...homestead lights and the old fields tilled by dead and gone generations who loved them," of being "home."

By 1939, the life of L. M. Montgomery was far from paradisal. Her health was no longer good, and her spirits very depressed. She was deeply distressed by the coming war. Her husband's ill health was a great worry. She was in correspondence with the Ryerson Press, which planned a Canadian edition of her earlier works. Ryerson had been agents for the old Page Company of Boston; now they were bringing the early books out again in Canada. There would be no change in the royalty arrangements. The whole business revived L. M. Montgomery's resentment over what she considered the exploitation of her efforts by the publishers. Two movie versions of *Anne* had been made, and two three-act plays based on *Anne* appeared in 1937, one by Alice Chadwicke, one by Wilbur Braun. Both, issued by French in New York, brought no returns to L. M. Montgomery, for she had sold all "rights" to dramatic versions for a lump sum back in 1907. She brooded also over the "piracy" suits she had suffered through in the twenties. Illness and depression grew together. She wrote to a correspondent who had paid her a tribute in 1940, "It always gives me pleasure to hear that [my books] have given a little help or enjoyment to my readers. Certainly in the kind of world that this has become we need all the help we can get."

L. M. Montgomery died April 24, 1942. She was buried in Cavendish, in the loveliness

Of cool, far hill, and long remembered shore,
Finding in it a sweet forgetfulness
Of all that hurt before.

Her husband died a year later. In Prince Edward Island, a stone monument has been erected at the entrance to Cavendish National Park, and the old "Green Gables" house, near L. M. Montgomery's childhood home, stands as a shrine to her memory and a recognition of the continuing reality of "Anne."

Her death brought a wave of retrospective articles, mostly nostalgic. Her old correspondent, Ephraim Weber, prepared two articles for the *Dalhousie Review*, "L. M. Montgomery as a Letter Writer," October, 1942, and " L. M. Montgomery's 'Anne,' " April, 1944. They remained the major serious contribution to knowledge of the author for many years. Subsequent critics of Canadian literature — such as Arthur Phelps in *Canadian Writers* (*1951*), and Desmond Pacey in *Creative Writing* (*1952*), were patronizing and casual. They spoke of her naïve plotting, her whimsy, her sentiment. Hilda M. Ridley's biography, *The Story of L. M. Montgomery* (*1956*), blurred some details, and over-emphasized the childhood background of the author. Wilfrid Eggleston in his graceful edition (1960) of *The Green Gables Letters* (*From L. M. Montgomery to Ephraim Weber, 1905-1909*), has done much to restore our sense of the wisdom and wit of this "lively and attractive personality."

Her established audience — girls between ten and fourteen — continues to read and love the L. M. Montgomery books. But she may also lay increasing claim to our attention as adult critics. The books have an intensity because they *were* written as "children's books." The same kind of sesame that unlocked Lewis Carroll's inhibitions and let him write the classic of fantasy and repression that we now see in *Alice* — that same magic releasing power seems to have operated with the Canadian, late-Victorian, provincial spinster. Writing "for children," she could re-enact the rituals of childhood. Recreating her own remembered yearnings and anxieties, she could create a myth of the hesitant desires and worries of the virginal years.

Modern psychology explains some of the hidden power of L. M. Montgomery's books, especially for adolescent girls.[2] Most teen-aged girls find it hard to get along with their mothers, the psychologists say, yet not daring consciously to dislike the mother, they are torn by mixed emotions of admiration, rivalry, dependence, hostility, all operating at a subconscious level. The heroines of L. M. Montgomery have no mothers. They do have aunts and grandmothers (who can safely be hated). Indeed, they usually have a range of aunts, some restrictive, some permissive. The adolescent reader can discriminate ambivalent feelings by loving one aunt (mother-substitute), while hating another. Also, in adolescence there is a normal intensity of feeling for the father, a feeling that must be outgrown or re-directed, but that is very powerful in the transitional stage between family relations and extra-familial ones, and correlates with the transition from homosexual to

24

heterosexual devotion. In most of L. M. Montgomery's books, the father, safely distanced by death, stirs deep feelings of attachment (usually disapproved of by the aunts or grandmothers).

Other tenets of the psychologists who study adolescence can similarly be illustrated from the Montgomery books. "Girls may feel unconscious jealousy of boys": in the novels girls replace boys, as Anne replaced the asked-for boy orphan, as Valancy replaced her mother's desired son. Many times, also, names are used to suggest crossing of boundaries:"Peter"in *The Quarantine* is a girl;"Bev,"the boy-narrator in the Story Girl series has an ambivalent name, as have "Phil", "Jo", Jamesina, Pat, and a long list of others. The theory would be that reading such tales gives young girls an outlet for their fantasies of changing sex. Another tenet: ''The adolescent longs for yet dreads the coming of physical passion.'' No doubt this accounts for the pleasure girls find in reading the long, long sequence of tales in which consummation of a romance is suspended, usually by some illogical tabu. Item: ''The ending of virginity may be symbolically accepted in dreams, as a prelude to reality.'' Re-reading the L. M. Montgomery books with even a reserved acceptance of Freudian symbolism would surprise most of us! Once again, the theory is that such gentle, sublimated acceptance into the young reader's consciousness can be a healthy form of gradual adjustment. Such a Freudian re-reading, besides increasing our interest in the ''Anne'' and ''Emily'' books, may lead to a revaluation of *The Blue Castle*, where many of the suppressed themes are directly stated.

The basic assumption in this revaluation is that L. M. Montgomery was probably not conscious of the forces she was releasing. She was, however, honest enough to use the patterns her memory suggested. Furthermore, she was a good enough craftsman to lift the stories from the level of clinical confession to that of archetypal statement.

We may guess, also, that this author was increasingly conscious of the basic equation she had established, almost by chance, in her first successful novel. ''The Island'' is adolescence. And Adolescence, that time of intense dreaming, of romantic yearning and disturbing hostility, remains as a part of every consciousness. Encircled by the mature sands of logic, pragmatism, utilitarianism and conformity, the island of youth exists for us and in us still. Perhaps art can be the channel by which we rediscover the island. L. M. Montgomery's world of poetry, virginity, and pantheism still opens for the adult reader the way back to his own world of young realization: he ''wakes, to dream again.''.

This brings us to the final claim of L. M. Montgomery on our attention and respect. She is the novelist for the bookish child, the word-conscious child to whom she gives reassurance about a sense of the magic of 'naming.' She knows that words are her tool, and have been so ever since as a child, by naming, she made her own Island in time.

NOTES

[1] This article is reprinted, by permission, from *The Clear Spirit*, ed.

Mary Quayle Innis (University of Toronto Press, 1966), pp. 198-219. The endnotes are an addition to the original.

[2] *The Road To Yesterday*, published earlier this year by McGraw - Hill Ryerson, presents further very interesting grounds for comment on the psychological aspects of L. M. Montgomery's vision.

Elizabeth Waterston, an Associate Editor of CCL and Chairman of the English Department at the University of Guelph, has written widely on Canadian literature. Two of her books are Composition for Canadian Universities *and* Survey: A Short History of Canadian Literature.

Satire, Realism, and Imagination in

Anne of Green Gables

MARY RUBIO

I t is interesting to speculate on what aspects of *Anne of Green Gables* have brought forth such a continuingly favourable response from so many people of varying ages and locales, with different degrees of literary sophistication. Certainly, this first novel by L. M. Montgomery put Prince Edward Island on the North American literary map.[1] Published by the Page Company in New York in 1908, the novel was an instant success: 10% royalties of the first six-month's worth of sales brought Montgomery $1,730--no small figure then. By 1930 it had been translated into French, Dutch, Swedish, and Finnish and had sold well over a million copies. Conceived as an adolescent novel, *Anne of Green Gables* surprised its author by appealing to young and old alike. In her letters to Ephraim Weber, Montgomery notes that the *Bookman* listed *Anne* as one of the six best-sellers in ten different major cities. Also, she summarizes the substance of a number of some sixty initial reviews, fifty-five of which are favourable. She tells Mr. Weber that Bliss Carman wrote a "flattering epistle" about the novel, but the greatest honour was receiving a letter from one of North America's most famous authors, Mark Twain, who wrote her "that in Anne I had created 'the dearest, and most lovable child in fiction since the immortal Alice'."[2]

One of the only negative reviews of *Anne* appeared in the *New York Times*. The reviewer stated that the novel had "A mawkish, tiresome impossible heroine, combining·the sentimentality of an Alfred Austin with the vocabulary of a Bernard Shaw."[3] (It boggles the imagination to speculate on Shaw's response to any inference that he and Anne Shirley were at the same vocabulary level.) One thing is certain--had this reviewer been correct in his assessment of the novel, Montgomery would *not* have received such praise from Mark Twain. For in his own immensely popular novels of boyhood (*Tom Sawyer,* 1876; *The Adventures of Huckleberry Finn,* 1884,) Twain had directed devastating satire at any attitude or literary work which smacked of overblown romanticism or sentimentality. Furthermore, as Twain grew older, he had suffered a number of personal and financial tragedies and, whether because of these or because of a deepening philosophical disillusion-

27

ment with mankind in general, his pessimism evolved into despair and bitterness, as anyone who reads his *Autobiography* and later writings will note. It is not easy to envision him in 1908, just two years before his death at age 75, as a mellow and kindly doddering old gentleman who was in the habit or writing encouragement to unknown, aspiring authors--especially if they were writing sentimental fiction, a mode he particularly disliked. Whatever criticism may be directed at *Anne*, one cannot dismiss it as typical of the overblown romantic fiction which was churned out for the popular markets of the day, the genre in which the *New York Times* reviewer puts it.

Romanticism as a serious literary mode had been falling into critical disfavour in America since as early as 1860. Although there was a continuing flood of extremely sentimental popular literature well through the turn of the century, major literary figures such as Mark Twain, William Dean Howells, and Henry James were writing realistic novels which attempted to reflect the actual details of life in their times. Some of the serious writers who were contemporary with L. M. Montgomery were carrying literary realism to the extreme of naturalism; she mentions reading (and disliking) Upton Sinclair's *The Jungle*.[4] It was in such a literary climate that Twain--arch-enemy of sentimentalism, one of literary romanticism's degenerate offshoots-- singled out *Anne of Green Gables* as a novel worthy of praise.

Montgomery's publisher brought out Eleanor H. Porter's best-selling novel *Pollyanna* four years after *Anne of Green Gables*. On the surface, their heroines may appear comparable: both Anne and Pollyanna believe in the power of positive thinking. But *Pollyanna*, temporarily popular though it was, is an excellent example of a sentimental tear-jerker. The realism and genuine characterization in *Anne* become very apparent by comparison.

It is likely that Twain responded to Montgomery's novel partly because of its realism in presenting Anne and the psychological relationships between her and the external world. In addition, one can assume that an important factor in his response was his recognition of Montgomery's treatment of a socio-religious climate he knew well--small town Scotch-Presbyterianism. She, like he himself in both *Tom Sawyer* and *Huckleberry Finn*, had used hypocritical and distorted religious views and behaviour as the serious basis for comedy.

Both he and Montgomery shared the comic touch of the ironist. Very like Twain's hometown of Hannibal, L. M. Montgomery's hometown of Cavendish (fictionally depicted as Avonlea) was a small town inhabited by dignified and rigid Scotch-Presbyterians, upon whose character she maintained considerable perspective. She wrote Weber in March 1908 that she wondered if "religion has been a curse or a blessing to the world." In a delightful ironic sketch in the same letter, she describes

> an old lady who is one of the sweetest creatures alive. She would not harm a fly and I have seen her weep bitterly over the sufferings of a wounded cat. But it puts her in a simple fury to

28

even hint that a merciful and loving God will hardly burn for all eternity the great majority of his creatures. I cannot understand this attitude on the part of so many. Nothing seems to enrage some people so much as any attempt to take away or mitigate their dearly beloved hell.[5]

Having grown up in a small Calvinistic town himself, Twain knew well the personality which has a contradictory split between natural kindness and religious sternness. Such characters he depicts well in Tom Sawyer's Aunt Polly and Huck's well-meaning tormentor, Miss Watson.

Both Montgomery and Twain had grown up with exposure to a distinctive variety of "Sunday school literature," a genre of 18th and 19th century writing which pretended to record the short life-history and sayings of child saints who lived perfect lives and died young, often after much suffering. Such literature, which had grown originally out of the Puritan concern for children's souls, was given *raison d'être* by the fact that infant mortality rates were so high. The Methodist and Sunday School movements of the 19th century prolonged the distribution of this type of children's literature, and the moralism present in it is also present in much of the secular fiction of the 19th century. It is reasonable to suspect that Twain's original impetus to create "bad" boys who steal and lie, but who are likeable in spite of their "sins" was the result of a childhood overdose of fictional "good" boys whom he found unpalatable. L. M. Montgomery comments that reading about little earthly saints convinced her that she could never be as good as they, so she might as well not try. Her own "favourite Sunday book . . . a thin little volume entitled *The Memoir of Anzonetta Peters* " obviously made quite an impression on her, but she says "I don't think that it had a good effect on me." However, she muses, "I shall never forget that book. It belonged to a type now vanished from the earth--fortunately--but much in vogue at that time. It was the biography of a child who at five years became converted, grew very ill soon afterward, lived a marvelously patient and saintly life for several years, and died, after great sufferings, at the age of ten." One of Anzonetta's characteristic trademarks was responding to any remark by quoting a verse of scripture or hymn stanza. Montgomery notes with some humour that she herself "dared not use verses and hymns in current conversation" for she "had a wholesome conviction that I should be laughed at." [6]

Such similarities in background may be responsible for the many ways in which Montgomery's and Twain's novels resemble each other. In each the central tension derives from the difference in perception between the adult and the child. The first character we meet in *Anne* is Mrs. Rachel Lynde, her house appropriately positioned where she can witness everything that goes on in the village. Montgomery presents her as the norm in the village, and Marilla is caught unwillingly in the middle trying to bring Rachel and Anne Shirley closer together in perception of acceptable behaviour. Anne, maturing, brings her own perspectives more in line with those of the village by the end of the novel, and Mrs. Lynde becomes less rigid. Likewise, Tom Sawyer and his Aunt Polly as well as Huck Finn and the Widow Douglas (and Miss Watson) have perspectives which are at odds with each other.

Montgomery emphasizes the imaginative nature of the child-vision, whereas Twain focuses on its innocence; but whichever the focus, the child and the adult view the world from very different vantage points.[7] And, it is from this discrepancy in viewpoint that the humour and the reality in each novel arise.

For instance, both authors show the adult vision of the world to be partly rooted in the Calvinistic Scotch-Presbyterian framework. Adults in all three novels are a relatively humourless bunch who take themselves and their lives very seriously. They distrust pleasure and frivolity, even if it is manifested in such harmless things as puffy sleeves and flowers on Sunday hats. The sparse, bare room which Anne enters at Green Gables reflects the no-frill nature of Marilla's personality, and Montgomery contrasts the icy-white of the room with Anne's perception of the glorious white of nature's blossoms outside.

At the beginning of *Anne*, Matthew is clearly the product of a repressive society: his personality is locked, inarticulate, within him. He is not afraid merely to express his opinions, he is afraid even to have them. During his four-year association with Anne, her spontaneity and love gradually draw him out, and his final fulfillment before his death comes in his being able to articulate his love for her in words. The simplicity of his words makes them even more touching: "Well now, I'd rather have you than a dozen boys, Anne . . . It was a girl--my girl--that I'm proud of"(p. 311).[8]

In *Tom Sawyer* it is Aunt Polly who gives Tom little .indication, verbal or otherwise, that she truly values and loves him. Though she is an extremely kind person, the natural and the spontaneous are repressed in her. She does cruel things to Tom in the belief that he will be bettered by a little suffering; worse, she fails to express her love for him. Only when she believes him dead does she express the extent of her affection. Fortunately for him and their future relationship, Tom has the emotional satisfaction of seeing her weeping for him.

Twain and Montgomery criticize the way religion is practised at various points in their works. Anne remarks that ''Some people are naturally good, you know, and others are not. I'm one of the others. Mrs. Lynde says I'm full of original sin." Later she tells Marilla "When I'm with Mrs. Lynde I feel desperately wicked and as if I wanted to go and do the very thing she tells me I oughtn't to do....Do you think it's because I'm really bad and unregenerate?" (p. 269) Fortunately, these spiritual worries don't oppress Anne's lively nature long. Tom Sawyer and Huck Finn--expecially Huck--are not so fortunate: Huck labours under his conscience throughout the whole novel as he tries to reconcile the position of religious yet slave-holding adults with his own naive and supposedly 'wicked' view that being cruel to Negroes is wrong. Finally his "sound heart and deformed conscience" lead him to choose going to Hell as the result of freeing a slave above accepting the religious hypocrisy of adults.

Likewise, the matter of prayers gives Montgomery and Twain a source of more comedy. When scolded by Marilla for failure to say her prayers, Anne replies, "Mrs. Thomas told me that God made my hair red *on purpose*, and I've never cared about Him since. And anyhow I'd always be too tired at night to bother saying prayers. People who have to look after twins can't be expected to say their prayers" (p.54). Anne's practical and childishly literal approach to prayer is reminiscent of Huck's: as he tells it, Miss Watson "told me to pray every day, and whatever I asked for I would get it. But it warn't so. I tried it. Once I got a fish-line, but no hooks. It warn't any good to me without hooks."

Some of the funniest incidents in both *Anne* and *Tom Sawyer* grow out of the adult conviction that a certain amount of suffering and humiliation in punishment is good for children. Anne's apology to Mrs. Lynde (p. 78) becomes unacceptable even though it is a very sincere apology because Anne enjoys delivering it. She becomes so caught up in doing it well with big words and dramatic gestures that she positively enjoys her own performance as one does an onerous task done well. Clearly it is not the act of apology, or the repentance it represents, but the suffering attendant upon it which is important. Likewise, had Aunt Polly realized the way in which Tom turned fence white-washing into a task full of positive enjoyment as well as profit, she would have been outraged rather than pleased at his cleverness and ingenuity. In each case humour comes through the reader's recognition that the adult position is slightly unreasonable; thus the situation becomes comic when the children outmaneuver the adults. There is delightful comic irony evoked by any such situation.

Thus, religion serves behind the scenes as a basis for humour: the religious background is the source of much of the tension in the novel, tension upon which the surface comedy can be built. It is the discrepancy between the outlandish behaviour of child heroines and heroes (Tom, Huck, Anne Shirley) and the acceptable norm in a quite small town (St. Petersburg and Avonlea) which creates the humour. Although childhood spontaneity can be repressed by many factors other than by distorted religiosity, in these three novels the adult perspective to a large extent results from a code of behaviour established by the literalism of small town and small-minded churchgoers.[9] Neither Twain nor Montgomery attack religion: they use distortions of it for comedy. But to dwell any longer on aspects of religious satire in Anne would be to distort the focus of Montgomery's work.

Both Montgomery and Twain, writing from mature perspectives, treat their respective communities and characters with humour and affection. Each had an eye for the incongruous, the comic dimension in human behaviour which results when adults and children alike take themselves too seriously and affect pompousness in language or action. Montgomery makes use of the difference between Anne's level of diction and her level of understanding: Anne's phrases, taken from her reading of sentimental fiction apparently, far exceed her level of maturation and understanding. Likewise, Tom Sawyer's imagination also is full of many undigested novels about pirates and robbers. *Huck Finn*, a much more complex work, uses a slightly converse situation. Huck's verbal abilities are moderate, but, naive as he may seem, his level of intuitive understanding is high. In each case, the reader is

31

aware of the ironic contrast between level of diction and level of comprehension, a contrast which achieves both humour and satire.

Both authors enjoy setting their characters in formal, ritualistic situations and then deflating the ritual with a grossly inappropriate but plausible event. Marilla's dignified meal for the stylish Mr. and Mrs. Chester Ross is devastated by Anne's horrified shriek that the pudding sauce being served is one from which she had removed a drowned mouse earlier in the day. Likewise, in Twain, people fall accidentally into graves during the most solemn moments, dogs howl in the middle of pompous funeral orations, interminable church services are disrupted by the yelps of unfortunate dogs who sit on pinching bugs, and so on.

Aside from *Anne's* comic and satiric elements, what has been responsible for its initial and continuing success? In spite of parallels between *Anne* and Twain's two novels of boyhood, Montgomery's work owes its success to elements distinctively its own: Anne is not a female Twain character. There are, in Anne, other areas which deserve comment: Montgomery's combination of realism and romanticism, her treatment of the imagination, and her perceptive dealing with the psychological needs of humans, both children and adults.

Anne of Green Gables is best considered as an example of literary realism, despite the fact that it contains such elements as haunted woods which are typical of romance. One of the realities which children can build up is a world of imaginative romance and dreams, and we must keep in mind that most of the highflown romance in *Anne* exists because Anne creates it in her mind. Her imagination takes over early in the book, and it is primarily from her point-of-view that we see much of Avonlea. She may be a pretentious little girl who has read too much without digesting it, but as such she represents a type of precocious adolescent who is familiar and realistic. Montgomery places her in a specific and realistic setting, and we finish the book with a good sense of what it was like to be a child living in a small Prince Edward Island town around 1900.

Anne Shirley uses the worst sentimental clichés when she talks. These serve a greater function than to create humour or to characterize her, however: through Anne's overly dramatic and flowery speech, Montgomery is able to satirize romance. Montgomery, writing of her own childhood, tells us that she was brought up with such "Literary pablum" as *Godey's Lady's Book,* which she always "devoured ravenously, crying my eyes out in delicious woe over the agonies of heroines who were all superlatively good and beautiful." [10] Montgomery, who also spent a considerable amount of her own time doing hack writing for money, was obviously quite aware of the distinction between fresh and hackneyed expression. Anne's overripe diction is clearly intended to be comic, not only because it is inappropriate speech for a girl her age, but also because it is very trite and hackneyed in itself. Montgomery is clearly satirizing the popular literary taste for sentimental cliches just as Twain does in *Huck Finn* when he exposes us to the poetry of sweet little dead Emmeline Grangerford, poetry which outdoes the worst of the sentimental female versifiers who were then popular. [11]

L. M. Montgomery was a highly disciplined and efficient writer who was, in some of her other novels, too aware of her reading public, and too willing to conform to their taste so as to sell. She turned out a great amount of material which she herself seems to consider "hack" work in her letters to Weber. The general tone of her letters to him indicates that she was quite gratified by the money which her pen brought, but she had no illusions that she was creating great literature in the stories and poetry which she ground out before and after *Anne* for the Sunday school magazines. She wrote him that she hoped her novels would sell so that she could quit the "Sunday School stuff": she had learned to cater to the public taste to satisfy publishers and as a financial necessity. When Weber complained that he did not like two things about *Anne of Green Gables*, namely Anne's superlative success in school and Matthew's death, Montgomery replied that she didn't either, but that she felt they would be demanded by the reading public, the first as a reward because Anne had been a good girl, and the second to enforce a choice upon Anne. When the publishers asked her for an immediate sequel to the immensely successful *Anne*, Montgomery immediately churned one out, but observed that it lacked the spontaneity and freshness of the first Anne book.

Perhaps another of the factors which has made *Anne of Green Gables* so successful both with adults and children is Montgomery's treatment of the imagination. The term "imagination" was a prominent one in the 18th and 19th centuries. By the time Montgomery used the term, it had become quite ambiguous through application to many contexts. At its worst it had come to mean pure escapism; at its best, it was a faculty by which man ordered the world into a complex set of symbols, both verbal and spatial, and determined his own relationship to them. To have an imagination (then and now) designated an ability to create dimensions to one's internal landscape into which one could go, alone or with companions, to explore fully the meaning of being human; it was a place where one ordered sensory experience to give it meaning; where one came to terms with himself, determined his own identity, and emerged as a human being with a vision more profound.

The term "imagination" is one of the key words and concepts in *Anne of Green Gables*. What, however, does Montgomery mean when she speaks of it?

Anne possesses imagination in both the worst and the best of senses. When we first meet her she retreats to imaginary worlds from an unhappy real world. But she also possesses an unique ability to take ordinary sensory data from the external landscape of Avonlea and arrange it within her own imagination into a fascinating world. Whereas Anne looks through a window and sees a world that is "wonderful" outside, Marilla looks through the same window at the same time and sees only a big tree that "blooms great, but the fruit . . . [is] small and wormy." Most people are very much influenced by the constructions which other people place on reality; a political orator, a popular singer, an evangelist--each can completely catch us up in his own perception of

33

reality. We can enter his imagination and see the world defined by his mood and by his particular arrangment of symbols. Some people perceive the world as a place of great struggle and probable defeat for them; external objects in their environment become threats. Other people regard the world as a challenge and a pleasure; the same factors which threatened the first group are a stimulus to the second. Anne Shirley possesses a perception of the world close to the second: readers love her for it.

The "imagination" has been much maligned by religion. Certainly we can see Marilla's distrust of it: "I don't believe in imagining things different from what they really are," she says; "When the Lord puts us in certain circumstances He doesn't mean for us to imagine them away" (p. 59). What Marilla's literal mind fails to discern is the difficulty of determining how things *really* are in reality. The external world does not exist for us until our senses gather data and our minds interpret it. Marilla might well reflect that a literal reading of the Bible tells us that one of the first requirements which God made of man after creation was that man use his imaginative faculty to name the animals which He had created.

Like Adam, Anne Shirley's first important act after coming to Avonlea is to rename the external world which she finds. "The Avenue," a stretch of blooming apple trees, is rechristened "the White Way of Delight," and "Barry's Pond" becomes "The Lake of Shining Waters." The names she chooses show us the particular quality of her perception of reality. She takes the commonplace and makes it beautiful. Marilla and Matthew do not have enough literary sophistication to realize that the particular phrases which Anne chooses to externalize her vision are somewhat hackneyed--they are merely enchanted with the positive nature of the vision itself.

Anne's stay in Avonlea is a fascinating study of how one's imaginative perception of the world can in effect metamorphosize the actual structure of the world. One of the most exciting and satisfying aspects of the novel is Anne's transformation of an ordinary farm into a fairyland and of an inarticulate old bachelor and a cheerless old maid into people who can articulate their love.

Dour old Aunt Josephine Barry, in her selfish way, speaks for many readers when she summarizes her responses to Anne: "She makes me like her because she is interesting." Most humans are a little short on imagination and, like Aunt Josephine, enjoy being lifted out of commonplace lives by a free spirit like Anne.

I think that ultimately what readers respond to in *Anne* is not the mementary, amusing diversion of Anne's imaginative flights of fancy, but rather something far more powerful--the recognition that our perception of reality often becomes the blueprint for our lives. Our expectations can create our future. One excellent study of this phenomenon occurs in Henry James' *The Turn of the Screw* . Whether evil ghosts exist at the beginning of the story we cannot be sure; in fact, we may doubt that they do. But certainly by the end of the story we can

see that the truth about their existence is irrelevant; the governess believes so positively in them that evil in fact is produced. As one James'
critic put it: "Fear is like faith: it ultimately creates what at the first it
only imagined." [12]   Anne herself is aware of the importance of one's own
perception of reality. She says "I read in a book once that a rose by any
other name would smell as sweet, but I've never been able to believe it.
I don't believe a rose *would* be as nice if it was called a thistle or a skunk
cabbage"(p. 42).

That the vision of the individual imagination gave existence and
shape to the external world was a tenet of literary romanticism; it is also,
in the 1970's , an idea being explored by modern psychologists who have
demonstrated, for instance, that a child who perceives himself as a
failure is quite likely to become one, no matter how great his native
abilities may be. But in 1908 when *Anne of Green Gables* appeared,
such a doctrine ran counter to the sociological and biological
determinism of the age. Other contemporary literary heroines of serious
adult fiction had little or no ability to control the direction of their lives.
Maggie, in Stephen Crane's *Maggie, A Girl of the Streets*   (1896), is
doomed by her environment from the beginning; Dreiser's heroine in
Sister Carrie (1900,1912) is a "little soldier of fortune," buffeted by fate
and forces totally beyond her control. In an intellectual climate where
people were presented as helpless either because of their own biological
make-up or because of the social atmosphere in which they lived, novels
such as *Anne of Green Gables* suggested that one's imagination could
influence the external world.

Today, children of the Anne Shirley age (11-15 in the novel) are
beginning to test their wings outside the family. They can watch Anne
manipulate her environment.   When she first meets Marilla and
Matthew they are most unpromising parents; all humanity in them
seems to be repressed, and what is more, they don't want her because
she is a girl.   Yet, they are better than the alternative, and Anne
determines to find warmth and human kindness in them. At first, her
manipulations are obvious -- she tells Matthew and Marilla that she is an
orphan that nobody ever loved and that she expects to be treated as
badly by them as by everyone else.   But her ability to control her
environment is achieved by far more than such obvious manipulation:
she presents herself as an interesting and impulsive child, one the
Cuthberts need because she can furnish them with the psychological,
emotional, and imaginative dimensions which are lacking in their own
lives. And she does the same for us, the readers.

NOTES

[1]She apparently put Canada on the map for at least one
reviewer. In her letters to Wilfred Eggleston (*The Green Gables
Letters*, ed. Eggleston, Ryerson, 1960, p. 72), L. M. Montgomery
recounts with some amusement that reviewer's comment: "What most
impresses an American is how these people of Canada *resemble ourselves*." "What," Montgomery muses, "did that poor man suppose we
were like down here [sic]???"

35

[2] The figures in this paragraph are taken from *The Green Gables Letters*, pages 85, 100, 81, 71-72, and 80.

[3] *The Green Gables Letters*, p. 72.

[4] *Letters*, p. 47.

[5] *Letters*, p. 63.

[6] L. M. Montgomery, *The Alpine Path* (Fitzhenry and Whiteside, reprint of 1917 edition), p. 50.

[7] Twain uses the satiric vision to show that childhood innocence is forever irreconcilable with adult corruption. Montgomery, on the other hand, seems to indicate that it is through the child's imaginative reinterpretation of the world and ensuing reconstruction of reality that the adult vision can be rectified and revitalized.

[8] All page references to the text of *Anne of Green Gables* are to the 1968 McGraw-Hill paperback edition.

[9] Two years before she wrote *Anne*, Montgomery was complaining to Weber about the restrictive orthodoxy of Cavendish: "Yes, I teach a Sunday School class--but I don't like it much. They never dream of asking a question, much as I have tried to induce them to, and all their idea of 'studying' a lesson seems to be to learn the printed questions in the quarterlies off by heart. I never can get them to give an answer in their own words and I don't believe they ever get one scrap of real good out of the lesson. I have to follow the old traditional paths of thought & expression or I would get into hot water immediately. Cavendish is wholesomely (?) old-fashioned and orthodox" (p.46).

[10] *The Alpine Path*, p. 48.

[11] At her worst, Montgomery herself could--and did--write florid, sentimental prose and verse. It seems very likely that in her treatment of Anne's use of language, she is consciously evaluating and satirizing a style which she herself used.

[12] Harold Goddard, "A Pre-Freudian Reading of *The Turn of the Screw*," quoted in the Norton Critical Edition of *The Turn of the Screw*, p. 198.

Mary Rubio, an Associate Editor of Canadian Children's Literature, *teaches North American and Children's Literature in the English Department at the University of Guelph. Together with Glenys Stow, she has completed an anthology of Canadian children's literature, intended for schools, which will be appearing in the spring.*

The Decline of Anne: Matron vs. Child

GILLIAN THOMAS

I t is a cliché of popular literature that sequels tend to be disappointing, and students of children's literature are all too sadly familiar with the decline of writers who turn themselves into human factories on the basis of a successful first book. After the phenomenal success of *Anne of Green Gables* in 1908, L. M. Montgomery wrote well over a dozen more books with a similar setting, five of which concentrate on Anne herself as the central character. Although these five other "Anne" novels are by no means without interest, they lack many of the qualities which make the first book so appealing. Montgomery herself described *Anne of Ingleside* (1939), which records Anne's life as the matronly mother of five children, as "just a pot-boiler",[1] and one doubts if she would have taken Anne as the main character for another novel even if her writing career had been prolonged further.

The progressively unsatisfactory nature of the five Anne sequels reveals a good deal about why their forerunner was so successful. Several important factors are missing from the grown-up Anne. When we meet the young Anne, she is an orphan sitting alone in a railway station. As most children's librarians know, "books about orphans", evoking, as they do, a mixture of pity and envy, enjoy an immense popularity among child readers. However, far from being alienated and unwanted, Anne in the later books is totally absorbed in a dense social network of family and rural community. Similarly, much of the young Anne's appeal to female readers stems from the substance of the book's initial episode, in which Anne is almost sent away because Marilla and Matthew had wanted a boy but the orphanage has sent Anne by mistake. In a world in which most female children rapidly become aware that they would have enjoyed a higher status both within the family and in the outside world had they been born male, this episode is bound to have a powerful effect on its readers. By contrast, the grown-up Anne enjoys (at second-hand) the social status of her doctor husband and willingly accepts the social restrictions which result from that role.

If the Anne of the first book is often considered a spirited individualist, then the Anne of the final book seems a rather dreary conformist. A somewhat priggish tone is established at the very beginning of *Anne of Ingleside* where, when Anne remarks to her old friend Diana that Marilla still makes red-currant wine ''in spite of the

37

minister and Mrs. Lynde . . . just to make us feel real devilish'', Diana giggles at the piece of wickedness and thinks that she ''did not mind 'devilish' as she would if anybody but Anne used it. Everybody knew Anne didn't really mean things like that. It was just her way.''[2]

One of the episodes in *Anne of Ingleside* which is most revealing of the adult Anne is the one in which her eight year old daughter, Di, becomes friendly with Jenny Penny, a new pupil at her school. Jenny's ''background'' is told to Anne by Susan, the Blythe family servant:

> They are a new family that have moved to the old Conway farm on the Base Line, Mrs. Dr. dear. Mr. Penny is said to be a carpenter who couldn't make a living carpentering . . . being too busy, as I understand, trying to prove there is no God . . . and has decided to try farming. From all I can make out they are a queer lot. The young ones do just as they like. He says he was bossed to death when he was a kid and his children are not going to be.[3]

Jenny, although a distinctly tougher character, has much of the storytelling ability of the young Anne and constantly fantasizes a more alluring family history for herself. Di is forbidden to go and stay overnight with Jenny because the Penny family are obviously ''unsuitable'' friends for the Doctor's children. When Di, at Jenny's instigation, sneaks away to the Pennys' house, she is appalled by its run-down appearance because she is ''accustomed to the beauty and dignity of Ingleside''. As the episode progresses, the Penny family fit more and more into the stereotype of the feckless working class and the sequence culminates with the terrified Di playing dead and being dumped outside Ingleside by the equally terrified Penny children. Interestingly, however, there is no hint throughout this episode that Jenny's storytelling has a source similar to the fantasies of the young Anne in a lonely childhood, or that her behaviour merits any response short of condemnation.

The first few chapters of *Anne of Ingleside* are taken up with the deadening and interminable visit of Gilbert's Aunt Mary Maria. The old woman is an intolerable prude and bully, but Anne, out of loyalty to Gilbert, is unable to exert pressure to persuade her to leave despite the fact that it is very clear that the situation is something of a nightmare for her:

> ''I feel as you do in dreams when you're trying to run and can only drag your feet,'' said Anne drearily. ''If it were only now and then . ... but it's every day. Meal times are perfect horrors now . . .''[4]

This Anne, who seems the willing victim of social convention, is bound to disappoint the readers who so admired the spirited Anne of the first book. The child who stamped her foot at Mrs. Lynde and who walked the ridge-pole for a dare has vanished and left in her place a woman intent on observing the social proprieties and for whom ''imagination'' has come to mean something which very closely resembles sentimentality.

Curiously enough, in the midst of its flights of sentimentality, the final "pot-boiler", *Anne of Ingleside*, and its predecessor, *Anne's House of Dreams*,[5] touch on much darker themes than the previous Anne novels. Anne's first baby dies. Her friend, Leslie Moore, lives out a death-in-life existence with her brain-damaged husband. Neither of these situations is permitted to become a permanent blight on the House of Dreams, however, for the stork (*sic*) brings Anne another child, and a highly contrived series of events, culminating in successful brain surgery, leads to the discovery that Leslie Moore's husband has been dead for many years and that "Dick Moore" is in fact her dead husband's amnesiac cousin. In *Anne of Ingleside* there is also the recurring theme of Anne's own death. Early in the novel, Anne's little son Walter, who is sent away in a state of mystification to stay with neighbours while his mother is due to give birth to another child, develops the obsession that she is dreadfully ill and likely to die. Naturally the episode ends cosily with hot milk, cookies and comfort being dispensed, but the same theme recurs soon after when Anne almost dies of pneumonia.

Amid these reminders of death, the final Anne novel contains two other very odd episodes. In the first of these, Anne "remembers" what happened at Peter Kirk's funeral. Kirk had evidently treated both his wives quite brutally and was generally disliked in the community. His first wife's sister, Clara Wilson, attends the funeral and delivers a tirade against the dead man:

> "He smiled when he told her after her little baby was born dead that she might as well have died too, if she couldn't have anything but dead brats. She died after ten years of it . . . and I was glad she had escaped him. I told him then I'd never enter his house again till I came to his funeral. Some of you heard me. I've kept my word and now I've come and told the truth about him. It *is* the truth . . . *you* know it" . . . she pointed fiercely at Stephen Macdonald . . . "*you* know it" . . . the long finger darted at Camilla Blake . . . "*you* know it" . . . Olivia Kirk did not move a muscle . . . "*you* know it" . . . the poor minister himself felt as if that finger stabbed completely through him.[6]

The truth of Clara Wilson's tirade is confirmed by the action of Kirk's widow:

> Olivia Kirk rose before her and laid a hand on her arm. For a moment the two women looked at each other. The room was engulfed in silence that seemed like a personal presence.
> "Thank you, Clara Wilson," said Olivia Kirk. Her face was as inscrutable as ever but there was an undertone in her calm, even voice that made Anne shudder. She felt as if a pit had suddenly opened before her eyes. Clara Wilson might hate Peter Kirk, alive and dead, but Anne felt that her hatred was a pale thing compared to Olivia Kirk's.[7]

This episode, the strangest and most powerful one in the novel, is immediately undercut by the "explanation" provided by Stephen Macdonald that Clara Wilson had been jilted in her youth by Peter Kirk. Thus the source of her hatred which was originally shown as outrage at her sister's suffering becomes instead the trivial vindictiveness of the jilted woman.

The novel, as a whole, ends on a muted note after an odd episode in which Anne believes that she is "losing" Gilbert to an old college acquaintance of theirs. They go to dinner with Christine Stuart, in whose company Gilbert is animated while having been quite remote and abstracted when with Anne. In the familiar Montgomery pattern, the darkness is quickly dispelled with the explanation that Gilbert's abstraction has been caused by his concern over a seriously ill patient who has now made a dramatic recover. The book ends with a determined celebration of marriage and family which remains curiously unconvincing.

Marian Engel has remarked that Margaret Laurence's novels, "unlike the sentimental novels of . . . L. M. Montgomery . . . pull no punches about their community."[8] This remark, taken in relation to some of the elements in the later Anne novels discussed here, leads to some interesting conclusions about the nature of L. M. Montgomery's writing. If "serious" literature tends to explore individual consciousness and awareness, then popular literature tends more frequently to celebrate social bonding. The re-union with the long-lost relative and the cunningly engineered marriage of true minds make up the familiar fabric of 19th century melodrama and "romantic" novels as well as of contemporary television soap opera.

If the young Anne's role is to transform Green Gables and its surroundings by the exercise of her "imagination", then the role of the grown-up Anne is more and more that of social engineer, bringing about the unions and re-unions on which popular literature is so dependent. Once she is married, Anne becomes an indefatigable matchmaker:

> "But they're all happy," protested Anne. "I'm really an adept. Think of all the matches I've made . . . or been accused of making . . . Theodora Dix and Ludovic Speed . . . Stephen Clark and Prissie Gardner . . . Janet Sweet and John Dougles . . . Professor Carter and Esme Taylor . . . Nora and Jim . . . Dovie and Jarvis . . . "[9]

Despite the incident at Peter Kirk's funeral which raises the spectre of sadism, and despite Anne's temporary apprehension that her own marriage may be failing, all of Anne's matches are presented as bringing about nothing short of perfect and permanent bliss for the objects of her schemes. The only one of her matches which goes awry does so because the couple she has marked out for one another have already secretly planned to marry, and thus her scheming is merely superfluous. The idea that some marriages can be unfulfilling or destructive is scarcely allowed to intrude on Anne's world. Similarly, while *Anne of Green Gables* and *Anne of Avonlea* incorporate and come to terms with some of the narrowness and petty meanness which is a familiar component of life in a small community, this element is more and more firmly thrust aside in the later Anne novels.

In part the shortcomings of the sequels to *Anne of Green Gables* develop naturally from the genre of the sentimental novel to which they belong. Their failings also spring from the social limitations on Anne Blythe who must behave appropriately for her role as "Mrs. Dr." It is a sad thought that, if the young Anne Shirley with her sharp eye for social hypocrisy were to meet her own grown-up self, she would probably not find that she was a "kindred spirit".

NOTES

[1] Quoted in Francis W. P. Bolger, *The Years Before 'Anne'* (Charlottetown: The Prince Edward Island Heritage Foundation, 1974), p. 207.

[2] L. M. Montgomery, *Anne of Ingleside* (Toronto: McClelland and Steward, 1939 repr .1972), p. 7. Subsequent references are to this edition.

[3] *Ibid.*, p. 190.

[4] *Ibid.*, p. 76.

[5] Although it immediately precedes *Anne of Ingleside* in terms of the course of Anne's life, *Anne's House of Dreams* was actually published twenty-two years earlier in 1917. Another Anne novel, *Anne of Windy Poplars,* which takes up Anne's life as a teacher before her marriage, was published in 1936.

[6] *Anne of Ingleside*, pp. 255-6.

[7] *Ibid* , p. 256.

[8] *The Globe and Mail*, Toronto, Saturday, April 19, 1975, p. 37.

[9] *Anne of Ingleside,* p. 102.

Gillian Thomas has taught children's literature at the University of Victoria, California State University, and Dalhousie University. She is presently teaching English at St. Mary's University while completing a book on the motif of the imaginary journey in children's stories.

Canadian Writers: Lucy Maud and Emily Byrd

ANN S. COWAN

Lucy Maud Montgomery considered herself a writer for the young although her books also engage adults, both those who encounter her works for the first time and those who reread books that delighted them as children. Since Montgomery intended her stories for young people, certain thematic and stylistic characteristics inevitably arise, but because these stories are children's *literature* the works have a lasting quality that survives the maturation of the reader and the passage of time.

When her friend and literary correspondent Ephriam Weber complained that Anne's success in school was "too extra-ordinary", Montgomery offered this explanation:

> . . . the book was written for *girls* and must please them to be a *financial* success. They would insist on some such development and I can't afford -- yet, at least -- to defy too openly the standards of my public. Someday I shall try to write a book that satisfies me wholly. In a book for the young it wouldn't do to have the hero "fail tremendously", as you say. They couldn't understand or sympathize with that. It would take older people. I do not think I'll ever be able to write stories for mature people. My gift such as it is·seems to lie along literature for the young. [1]

For her young audience she wrote tales with child-heroines who succeeded in winning respect from their peers and superiors though confronted with the problems all children face. Anne, for example, has great difficulty being "good", often meeting calamity through well-intentioned deeds. Both Emily and Anne are orphaned, a conscious or unconscious fear that most children experience. Children also worry about the future. L. M. Montgomery reassured her young readers in the sequels to *Anne of Green Gables, Emily of New Moon,* and *Pat of Silver Bush* that the heroine would grow up to find happiness and success. The unattractive and unloved would become beautiful and loved (*The Blue Castle*). Those who had lived with a grudge or whose lives had been stained by misunderstanding would eventually find peace and understanding (*A Tangled Web*).

In return for satisfying her audience, L. M. Montgomery achieved financial success. In *The Green Gables Letters,* an interesting collection of letters written to Ephriam Weber between 1905 and 1909, when she was enjoying her first steady success, Montgomery wrote of her progress selling poems to increasingly prestigious magazines and included bits of advice to Mr. Weber on how to "break in" to various magazines. "Breaking in" invariably involved writing for the audience of the particular magazine. Many of Montgomery's first stories were sold to Sunday school magazines and were tailored to their requirements, but her tailoring was not without misgivings as she complained in her diary:

> I like doing these, but I should like it better if I didn't have to drag a moral into most of them. They won't sell without it, as a rule. So in the moral must go, broad or subtle, as suits the fibre of the particular editor I have in view. The kind of juvenile story I like best to write -- and read, too, for the matter of that -- is a good jolly one, "art for art's sake" or rather "fun for fun's sake," with no insidious moral hidden away in it like a pill in a spoonful of jam! [2]

Many of Montgomery's "moralistic" stories were collected into *Further Chronicles of Avonlea* , republished after her death. She preferred the sort of story the Story Girl tells in *The Story Girl* and *The Golden Road.* These were folk tales and stories of fun and adventure, the kind Montgomery's Great Aunt Mary Lawson might have told. Emily of New Moon's tale, "The Woman Who Spanked the King", which wins Emily a job offer in New York, is one of Aunt Mary's stories. Montgomery's biographer, Hilda Ridley, claims that *The Story Girl* was her most personally satisfying work.

The sequels to *Anne of Green Gables* were written at the request of the publishers. Montgomery confessed to Weber in a letter dated September 10, 1908, that her new Anne book was not as artistically satisfying as the original. "The new book was", she claimed, "built rather than created".

> But I am really convinced that it is not so good from an *artistic* standpoint, though it may prove popular and interesting enough. . . . The publishers wanted this--and I'm awfully afraid if the thing takes, they'll want me to write her through college. The idea makes me sick. I feel like the magician in the Eastern story who became the slave of the "jinn" he had conjured out of a bottle. If I'm to be dragged at Anne's chariot wheels the rest of my life I'll bitterly repent having "created" her. [3]

Anne was the subject of six novels and eventually grew into the middle-aged mother of six children, one of whom was killed in World War One. In her last Anne book, we suspect L. M. Montgomery of murderous intentions when she makes Anne dangerously ill and suggests that her condition is feeble -- too feeble for any more books!

It is unfair to accuse Montgomery of rank commercialism. She was a craftsman and wrote well regardless of the inspiration. To dismiss as a pot-boiler (even though she might have called it so herself) any piece she wrote to satisfy her market suggests that a writer's serious thoughts are confined to works in which he allows his muse complete freedom. Writers are not always their own best critics nor is the market always the best judge or a writer's work. In Montgomery's case, her own favourite books, *The Story Girl* and *The Golden Road,* and the most popular, *Anne of Green Gables, Anne of Avonlea,* and *Anne of the Island*, are inferior, in my opinion, to the Emily books, and it is on the strength of these that Montgomery's reputation as a children's novelist must rest.

In *Emily of New Moon, Emily Climbs,* and *Emily's Quest,* L. M. Montgomery tempers the romantic fantasies of a book for girls with autobiographical notes from the life of a struggling young writer. The resultant trilogy fascinates the young reader and holds the interest of the adult. As Emily matures as a woman and as a writer, she must resolve the large questions of the human condition, and, in this, the books move into the realm of literature.

Because of their autobiographical nature, the "Emily" books hold a special interest for Montgomery's readers. She thoroughly disapproved of biographies and forbade her friend Weber to "write her life":

> So "if I die before you do, you'll write my life?" No, you won't!
> Nobody shall. . . . Biography is a *screaming farce.* No man or
> woman was *ever* truly depicted. Biographies, even the best, are
> one -- or at most two-sided -- and every human being has half a
> dozen different sides. It must always be that way until some
> medium of communication is found for "soul moods".[4]

The creation of Emily Byrd Starr afforded L. M. Montgomery an opportunity for a wide range of soul worlds. Since many of the facts of Emily's life correspond with Montgomery's own, perhaps we can assume that they shared as well a few of the "soul moods". Hilda Ridley suggests that such a liberty is not entirely misguided.

> Lucy Montgomery, without doubt, drew largely on her own
> experiences in all her work, but it should be remembered that to
> her the world of imagination was almost as real as that of
> concrete fact, and in drawing upon the events of her past life
> she often recorded episodes that belonged as much to this realm
> as to her ordinary, everyday life.[5]

Emily Byrd Starr's writer-father was much resented by the Murrays of Blair Water whose youngest daughter, Juliet, had disgraced herself by marrying. According to the Presbyterian ethic of Montgomery's milieu, writers are irresponsible dreamers (see *Jane of Lantern Hill* and *The Story Girl*) and earn only grudging respect when they achieve financial success. They are always adored by Montgomery's heroines for their sensitivity to suffering and joy and for their appreciation of nature (*Blue Castle*). Even their understanding of religion is different from the accepted social view. Emily contrasts "Father's God" with "Aunt Elizabeth's God". But the heroine always finds a society of "kindred souls" to compensate for the insensitivity of the larger society. As a fledgling writer Emily enters this hostile society, but is protected by the understanding of Dean Priest and Cousin Jimmy, and comforted by the memory of her writer-father. Both of her champions are also outsiders by virtue of infirmities which make them "different". Dean Priest suffers from a crooked back and Cousin Jimmy is considered "simple" because he hasn't been "quite right" since being pushed in a well as a child. Jimmy supplies Emily with note-books, a luxury in Presbyterian New Moon, and defends her before Aunt Elizabeth when she is attacked by a vindictive teacher.

The acknowledgement that society is not receptive to the poet marks a development in Montgomery's attitude to her young audience. Her earlier heroine, Anne, had a flair for writing too, and although Marilla scolded her occasionally, she never faced the hostility Emily encounters. Both Anne and Emily write wildly romantic tales and choose exotic names for their heroines. (A fault shared by L. M. Montgomery; see *The Story Girl* and *Chronicles of Avonlea*.) They both learn, however, to exercise artistic restraint. Anne is told to write only of what she knows and to criticize her own work sharply.[6] Emily's Mr. Carpenter, on reviewing all of her work, finds ten good lines. He becomes a stern critic of Emily's work, far beyond the role of teacher. Montgomery suggests in *Emily of New Moon* that the child writer is father unto the man-writer and as such must not be sheltered from the trials and hardships of life and literature -- a marked change from the Anne books. Mr. Carpenter says:

> I think there's *something* trying to speak through you -- but you'll have to make yourself a fit instrument for it. You've got to work hard and sacrifice -- by gad, girl, you've chosen a jealous goddess. And she never lets her votaries go -- not even when she shuts her ears forever to their plea.[7]

The writer writes because he is compelled to write. Anne's writing is the extension of her lively imagination but Emily's is a vocation. When Mr. Carpenter reads Emily's frank description of him, he exclaims, "By gad, it's literature, *literature* -- and you're only thirteen."[8] Mr. Carpenter tells Emily at the end of *Emily of New Moon* that she must climb: "If it's *in* you to climb you must -- there are those who must lift their eyes to the hills -- they can't breathe properly in the valleys." [9] *Emily Climbs* is the story of Emily's literary development through her teenage years, and *Emily's Quest* tells of her final conflict as she struggles to reconcile her vocation with the demands of womanhood.

Aside from their literary gifts, Emily of New Moon and Lucy Maud Montgomery share many similarities. Both were aware of death in early childhood. Emily's description of the death of her mother corresponds almost word-for-word with the description in Montgomery's biography of her childhood memory of her mother's death. Mr. Carpenter remarks on reading Emily's poetry that she "knows something of death", while Anne, though an orphan, is seemingly unaware of death except in her abstract imaginings. Emily and Lucy were both solitary children who imagined playmates. Emily held long conversations with "Emily-in-the-glass", and Lucy christened her reflection in the bookshelves "Katie Maurice". All children understand loneliness -- even if their only experience is the occasional exclusion from playground games. L. M. Montgomery offers her personal solution, a retreat into the imagination.

In her later books, Montgomery allows her heroines more suffering and consequently greater strength to overcome it. Anne is immediately loved and accepted by her schoolmates; Emily, like young Lucy, is teased about her high button boots and baby apron and persecuted because "you ain't a bit like us". Childhood prejudice is painful and it is a mark of Montgomery's literary progress that she skilfully copes with it in her later novels. The devotion of Anne and Diana is far less realistic than the stormy friendship of Emily and Ilse. Emily had "loved" Rhoda Stuart with the same sentimentality that colours Anne and Diana's friendship -- only to discover Rhoda unworthy. Emily's friendship with Ilse allows for Ilse's quick temper and Emily's stubborn pride.

Emily's discoveries about writing parallel her discoveries about life. In a sense her literary progress provides a framework for the three novels while her growing maturity supplies the supporting interest and detail. One of the most dramatic examples of the close relationship of personal and literary growth occurs in *Emily's Quest.* When Emily becomes engaged to marry Dean Priest, her cousin, friend, confidant, and critic from early childhood, she senses that her marriage will end her literary career. Dean has always praised her writing but has laughed at her for taking "these trifles" seriously. Since Dean saved Emily's life as a child he has always half-jokingly half-seriously claimed that her life belongs to him. Montgomery does not admit the right of one person to possess or dominate another, and characters who try to do so in her novels are always foiled. Teddy Kent's mother, in her attempt to possess her son, jealously discourages the friendship between Emily and Teddy. This conflict mirrors the Emily-Dean relationship.

Dean's greatest crime is to lie to Emily about her writing. In his jealousy of her work, he discourages Emily who, in faith, burns her first book. Emily agrees to give up her writing and marry Dean even though she loves someone else. Of course, Montgomery cannot let this happen. To change the course of events, she gives Emily the gift of "second sight". Emily is able, with this gift, to prevent Teddy from sailing on a boat that sinks. The incident makes Emily realize how close she is "spiritually" to Teddy and how wrong of her it would be to marry anyone else. Unfortunately, Emily's pride and Mrs. Kent's jealousy delay the mutual discovery of their love until many years later, but Emily learns two significant things. She cannot give up her writing nor can she deny her heart, both important aspects of L. M. Montgomery's own experience.

Anne does give up her writing. When Gilbert suggests that she has sacrificed, Anne replies that her family is more important than the "few children's stories" she wrote, an attitude Montgomery certainly never shared. Despite her busy life as a minister's wife and a mother, Montgomery always found time for her writing. She always acknowledged the right of both men and women to fulfill their destinies. "Sex", she maintained, "seems to me to enter very little into the question. There is no sex in mind, I do believe, and --'let each one find his own', and her own, in business as well as matrimony." [10]

One of the most striking qualities Emily shows is her compassion.

Even though Mrs. Kent has greatly wronged her, and even though Dean has lied to her, Emily is able to forgive them readily because she can see that pain and weakness have motivated them. Compassion was Mr. Carpenter's most valuable lesson. Carpenter saw himself in Emily's satire of old Peter DeGeer and chastized her sadly:

> There is a place for satire -- there are gangrenes that can only be burned out -- but leave the burning to the great geniuses. It's better to heal than hurt. We failures know that. . . . When *I* am dead say, "He was a failure, and none knew it more truly or *felt* it more bitterly than himself." Be merciful to the failures, Emily. Satirise wickedness if you must -- but pity weakness.[11]

Mr. Carpenter's last lesson is delivered on his death bed in *Emily's Quest*. He makes her promise that she will write to please only herself:

> Keep that -- and you'll be -- all right. No use trying to please everybody. No use trying to please -- critics. Live under your own hat. Don't be -- led away -- by those howls about realism. Remember -- pine woods are just as real as -- pigsties -- and a darn sight pleasanter to be in. You'll get there -- sometime -- you have the root -- of the matter -- in you. And don't -- tell the world -- everything. That's what the -- matter -- with our -- literature. Lost the charm of mystery -- and reserve.[12]

Neither Emily nor Montgomery write of pigsties, but Montgomery does write of pain with compassion and truth, romance tempered with the realism of experience. While Emily's lapse from the writer's faith is only temporary, it is an important element in her growth. Emily must justify her decision to write in her own fashion. While she has the moral courage to believe she is right, she must have some form of tangible success and finally the approval of her family. Predictably, this comes for Emily because of her maturity and compassion. When Aunt Elizabeth breaks her leg, Emily entertains her with daily chapters from a novel she writes. Aunt Elizabeth, who has always been highly suspicious of Emily's stories, does not disapprove of this story because the characters are so life-like it seems *true*. Aunt Elizabeth is determined that Nicholas Applegath is "too much like old Douglas Courcy of Shrewsbury", a gentleman Emily has never met. L. M. Montgomery faced similar problems:

> Ever since my first book was published . . . I have been persecuted by the question "Was so-and-so the original of such-and-such in your book?" . . . Now for my own part, I have never . . . met one human being who could, as a whole, be put into a book without injuring it. Any artist knows that to paint *exactly* from life is to give a false impression of the subject. *Study* from life, he must . . . "making use of the real to perfect the ideal". But the ideal, his ideal, must be behind and beyond it all. The writer must *create* his characters, or they will not be life-like.[13]

Both Emily and L. M. Montgomery received contradictory reviews. One of the most significant for Emily is the one from Janet Royal in New

York. Miss Royal had been angry when Emily refused her offer of a position in New York:

> What can you ever do here that is worthwhile, child? . . . You can't get material here -- there's no atmosphere.[14]

Emily replied that she would create her own atmosphere,

> And as for material -- people *live* here just the same as anywhere else -- suffer and enjoy and sin and aspire just as they do in New York . . . . Some fountain of living water would dry up in my soul if I left the land I love.[15]

Miss Royal's letter affirms Emily's understanding of the nature of her literary gift:

> You were right not to come to New York. . . . You could never have written the *Moral of the Rose* here. Wild roses don't grow on city streets. And your story is like a wild rose, dear, all sweetness and unexpectedness, with sly little thorns of wit and satire. It has power, delicacy, understanding. It's not just story-telling, there's some magicry in it. Emily Byrd Starr, where do you get your uncanny understanding of human nature -- you infant.[16]

Aunt Elizabeth pronounces the final dictum: "Well I never believed that such a pack of lies could sound as much like the real truth as that book does."[17]

The novel is justified, the *Canadian* novel is justified, and Emily has found success. L. M. Montgomery, in the Emily trilogy, has successfully expanded the themes of her novels for girls to create a work of literature that sensitively explores the problems and conflicts facing the young Canadian female novelist in a society which places a literary career second to the role of wife and mother. The work, though fiction, is successful in its truth-telling because Montgomery wrote from her own understanding of life and literature.

Her financial success and popularity are no more important than her place in Canadian literature as a novelist of the first rank. Canadians have paid tribute to L. M. Montgomery in their fashion. In 1935 King George V conferred upon her the decoration "Officer of the British Empire" (OBE). In the contest held by *The Family Herald and Weekly Star* (1925), she was declared second only to Charles Dickens in a list which included the greatest and most popular writers of the present and the past.[18] Her first and most famous novel *Anne of Green Gables* was performed as a musical at the opening of the Charlottetown Centre for the Arts and was part of Canada's display at the World Exposition in Japan, 1970. The Canadian National Railway has honoured her by christening one of its largest ships *Lucy Maud Montgomery;* on its daily run to Newfoundland, this vessel bears the name of Canadian letters on the high seas. And Canadian letters bear the name of Lucy Maud Montgomery in the form of an eight cent stamp, issued in honour of her centenary year.

[1] L. M. Montgomery, *The Green Gables Letters* ed. Wilfrid Eggleston (Toronto: Ryerson, 1960), p. 73.

[2] Hilda M. Ridley, *The Story of L. M. Montgomery* (London: Harrap & Co., 1956), p. 75.

[3] L. M. Montgomery, *The Green Gables Letters,* ed. Wilfrid Eggleston, p. 74.

[4] *Ibid.*, p. 58.

[5] Hilda M. Ridley, *op. cit.,* p. 93.

[6] L. M. Montgomery, *Anne of Green Gables* (Toronto: Ryerson, 1968), p. 272.

[7] L. M. Montgomery, *Emily of New Moon* (Toronto: McClelland and Stewart, 1923), p. 348.

[8] *Ibid.*, p. 349.

[9] *Ibid.*, p. 350.

[10] L. M. Montgomery, *The Green Gables Letters*, ed. W. Eggleston, p. 91.

[11] L. M. Montgomery, *Emily Climbs* (Toronto: McClelland and Stewart, 1925), p. 21.

[12] L. M. Montgomery, *Emily's Quest* (Toronto: McClelland and Stewart, 1927), p. 33.

[13] H. M. Ridley, *op. cit.,* pp. 95-6.

[14] L. M. Montgomery, *Emily Climbs*, p. 298.

[15] *Ibid.*, pp. 298-300.

[16] L. M. Montgomery, *Emily's Quest*, pp. 242-3.

[17] *Ibid.*, p. 248.

[18] From the dust jacket of the 1927 edition.

Ann S. Cowan is a project officer in the History Division of the National Museum of Man, Ottawa.

"Queer Children"
L. M. Montgomery's Heroines

MURIEL A. WHITAKER

W hen I was a child, the novels of L. M. Montgomery occupied half a
shelf in our glass-doored bookcase. First editions, mostly, they had
been inscribed to my mother and aunt by various gift-giving relatives. I
read them eagerly, supplementing our own holdings with others
borrowed from the public library, until I had gone through the *Anne*
books, the *Emily* books, *Kilmeny of the Orchard, The Story Girl* and the
rest. My own daughters, at a time when they were reading almost
nothing but horse stories, showed a similar enthusiasm for L. M.
Montgomery. Evidently she is one of those perennial authors whom
girls in their early teens cannot resist.

It was with some hesitation that I recently returned to *Anne of
Green Gables* (Boston, 1908), *Emily of New Moon* (Toronto, 1923), *The
Blue Castle* (Toronto, 1926) and *Pat of Silver Bush* (Toronto, 1933); a
hesitation stemming partly from reluctance to burst the bubble of nostalgia, partly from an awareness of critical disapproval. In her study of
Canadian children's literature, Sheila Egoff, while grudgingly accepting
the original Anne as a national institution, condemns "the increasingly
sentimental dishonesty of the succeeding books".[1] E. K. Brown is
equally disparaging about an author "who was satisfied to truckle to
mediocre taste".[2] On rereading, *Anne* seemed not at all bad and *Emily*
interested me so much I wanted to read the rest of the series to see how
things turned out. Admittedly, the charm was partly that of a period
piece. Canadiana is "in" at the moment: though we no longer use gin
jars for hot water bottles or keep up a parlour for serious occasions,
hooked rugs, patchwork quilts, and butter churns are highly prized and
highly priced. Is the appeal of L. M. Montgomery's novels simply a
matter of nostalgia or do they contain something of lasting, if minor,
literary value? In what context do her child heroines operate? What
makes Anne and Emily particularly interesting, and Valancy and Pat
less so?

When Mark Twain describes Anne as "the sweetest creation of
child life yet written,"[3] he is implicitly setting her in the context of English children's literature, a genre that originated with the Puritans in the
seventeenth century. Because the Puritan child was regarded as a
"brand of hell,"[4] it was the duty of parents, teachers, and guardians to
impress on him both the sinfulness of his fallen nature and the ideal

which he should follow if he would escape the fires of hell. Gratitude, duty, reverence, sobriety, humility, industry, and above all obedience were the desired virtues; vanity, impertinence, impiety, and disobedience were the faults which, in the didactic literature that adults thought suitable for children, inevitably led to horrendous ends. Transported to New England by the Pilgrim Fathers and to the Maritimes and Ontario by the Presbyterians, the Puritan ethic continued to affect the life and literature of Canadian and American children for many generations.

Marilla Cuthbert, Rachel Lynde and Mrs. Barry in *Anne of Green Gables*, and Ellen Greene, Aunt Elizabeth and Miss Brownell in *Emily of New Moon* are purveyors of the moral and religious ethos which controls the lives of Montgomery's heroines. It is a highly ritualised society, supported on the twin pillars of church and work. Labour in the rural community is determined by the cycle of the seasons; social intercourse, by the round of Sunday church, midweek prayer meeting, Ladies' Aid, and school. Propriety and conformity, a regard for "decency and decorum," prevail. Explanations must be found for uncharacteristic behaviour, a necessity that leads to the prying and gossiping that characterise any closely knit society. So Mrs. Rachel Lynde cannot rest until she finds out why Matthew Cuthbert, dressed in his best suit, is driving off in the middle of the afternoon when he should be sowing his late turnip seed in the big red brook field of Green Gables.

The odd and the out of place are immediately suspect. It is the queerness of Anne Shirley, both in physical appearance (bright red hair, wild flowers on her hat) and character (garrulity, imagination) that catches the eye and ear of Avonlea and of the reader. The orphaned Emily Starr is told that her Murray relatives won't like her because "you're queer, and folks don't care for queer children." One mark of her queerness is pointed ears, indicating that she is "kin to tribes of elf-land." (Calvinist orthodoxy combines with Celtic Fantasy in the world of Prince Edward Island). Even Anne's "bosom friend" Diana, an entirely conventional child in most respects, is set apart by the fact that she is named for a pagan goddess --"I'd ruther Jane or Mary or some sensible name like that," is Matthew's comment. Inevitably, Ilse Burnley's unconventional upbringing causes much head-shaking in the Blair Water community.

Almost as suspect as the odd is the beautiful, utility being preferred when it comes to making value judgments. Thus the blossoming cherry tree to which Anne responds so ecstatically is dismissed by Marilla:

> It's a big tree . . . and it blooms great but the fruit don't amount to much never - small and wormy.

Girl's dresses should be "good sensible, serviceable dresses, without any frills or furbelows" rather than the prettily fashionable garments with extravagant puffed sleeves that Anne longs to wear. The high buttoned shoes and "terrible" gingham sunbonnets and aprons in which Emily is dressed are models of utility and defences against vanity. The rigorous criteria regarding clothes extend also to reading material (novels are "wicked books and have ruined many souls"), to bangs, to

51

whistling. In fact, "a great many jolly things" are, if not wicked, at least unladylike.

The Puritan view required that the child should be taught by exhortation, example, and punishment. "Correction in itself is not cruel." Dr. Samuel Johnson had proclaimed. "Children, being not reasonable, can be governed only by fear. To impress this fear is therefore one of the first duties of those who have the care of children."[5] Mrs. Lynde has no hesitation in impressing on Anne that she is full of original sin and in recommending to Marilla the use of a switch. The fearful Calvinistic doctrine of election is apparent in Anne's view of herself:

> No matter how hard I try to be good I can never make such a success of it as those who are naturally good.

Attendance at Sunday school and church, saying one's prayers, learning to cook, clean, and make patchwork squares are all part of a proper bringing up. The adults provide sustenance, direction, and good example; the children are to respond in the way that Aunt Elizabeth expects:

> Emily, you must understand right now that you are to be grateful and obedient and show your appreciation of what is being done for you. I won't have tears and repining. What would you have done if you had no friends to take you in? Answer me that.

In spite of genuine effort on the part of the children, the old Eve will out. Vanity, disobedience, lying, anger, stubborness, pride, a regular Pandora's box of "viciousness," are illustrated by their careers. Yet unlike the children in the "horrendous example" school of literature, [6] these heroines do not come to a bad end. Rather, in the tradition of Rousseau's *Emile,* they learn by experience, as Anne realises:

> Ever since I came to Green Gables I've been making mistakes, and each mistake has helped to cure me of some great shortcoming. The affair of the amethyst brooch cured me of meddling with things that didn't belong to me. The Haunted Wood mistake cured me of letting my imagination run away with me. The linament cake mistake cured me of carelessness in cooking. Dyeing my hair cured me of vanity . . .

In the end, Anne conforms pretty closely to the adult view of propriety, a fact that makes her a much less interesting character in subsequent books.[7]

The Puritan idea of the child is not the only determiner of character in the novels of L. M. Montgomery. Combined with it is the idea of the child as innocent victim, orphaned, abandoned, often doomed to an early death. That this was a popular motif in Victorian literature the novels of Dickens, MacDonald, and Kingsley, among others, testify. The pathos of Anne and Emily depends to a considerable extent on the fact that they are orphans.[8] The awareness of deprivation is vividly illustrated by Emily's response to New Moon:

She felt utterly alone and lonely -- there in that darkness, with an alien, hostile world all around her -- for it seemed hostile now. And there was such a strange, mysterious, mournful sound in the air -- far away, yet clear. It was the murmur of the sea, but Emily did not know that and it frightened her. Oh, for her little bed at home -- oh, for Father's soft breathing in the room . . .

At the same time, their dramatisation of this awareness is psychologically convincing. Whenever Anne thinks it can benefit her, she reminds the critical adults -- Marilla, Mrs. Lynde, Mrs. Barry, Miss Josephine Barry -- that she is "a poor little orphan girl" whose mistakes result from ignorance rather than intention. As a member of the proud and successful Murray clan, Emily is not so rootless as Anne; she has a sense of belonging to a family group even though duty rather than love has motivated the Murrays' acceptance of her. On the other hand, while Anne is immediately popular with her classmates, Emily suffers at school for being a "proud" Murray and a stranger. "Why don't you like me?" she asks. "Because you ain't a bit like us," is the reply.

Isolation is the favourite punishment inflicted by Marilla and Aunt Elizabeth -- being banished to one's room, being forbidden to attend parties and picnics, being ostracized. When Emily refuses to kneel before the unjust teacher, Miss Brownell, and beg her pardon, Aunt Elizabeth tells her

> . . . you will be outcast in this house until you do. No one will talk to you -- play with you -- eat with you -- have anything to do with you until you have obeyed me.

The prospect is so horrifying to a sensitive child that she prefers the shame of yielding.

Eventually, the qualities which in the beginning tended to isolate them -- Anne's rootlessness and active imagination, Emily's pride and poetic gift -- provide them with the motivation to overcome misfortune and win acceptance. Anne's severest critic, Rachel Lynde, is forced to admit:

> . . . I did make a mistake in judging Anne, but it weren't no wonder, for an odder, unexpecteder witch of a child there never was in this world, that's what. There was no ciphering her out by the rules that worked with other children. It's nothing short of wonderful how she's improved these three years, but especially in looks . . .

Although Valancy Stirling, the heroine of *The Blue Castle* , is a twenty-nine year old spinster, she also is a type of rejected child. Her father having died, she has been brought up by her mother, Mrs. Frederich, and Cousin Stickles with the advice of assorted relations. All of them are proponents of the Puritan view of child-raising and all of them persist in treating Valancy as a child. An awareness of her loveless condition stems from the time when, at the age of the nine,

> she was standing alone on the school playground while the other

girls of her class were playing a game in which you must be chosen by a boy as his partner before you could play. Nobody had chosen Valancy -- little, pale, black-haired Valancy, with her prim, long-sleeved apron and odd, slanted eyes.

Valancy inhabits two homes: an ugly, red brick box on Elm Street and a Blue Castle in Spain where there are

courts, marble-pillared where shimmering fountains fell and nightingales sang among the myrtles; halls of mirrors that reflected only handsome knights and lovely women - herself the loveliest of all, for whose glance men died.

The likelihood that she will, in her state of sexual frustration, become completely unhinged, is aborted when she receives a doctor's letter informing her that she has a fatal heart disease that will carry her off within a year. Realising that she cannot be worse off than she is now --"I'm poor -- I'm ugly -- I'm a failure -- and I'm near death" -- she ticks off her relations and leaves home to keep house for the village drunk and his betrayed daughter who, having lost her illegitimate child, is now about to die of consumption (the wages of sin motif neatly combining with that of innocent victim).

Unfortunately, we can neither sympathise with Valacy nor admire her. The Castle in Spain fantasy, realised as an island retreat in the wilds of Ontario, is pure corn, but not less so is the heroine's marriage to frog prince Snaith who turns out to be not only the famous nature writer, John Foster, but also the son of a multi-millionaire Purple Pill producer (a fact that brings Valancy's disapproving relatives round in a hurry). Nor are we surprised to learn, after a Perils-of-Paulinish episode involving a shoe heel caught in a railway track before an onrushing train, that Valancy's fatal heart condition really belonged to another Sterling and that violet-eyed Barney has married Valancy out of love not pity. It is tempting to exculpate L. M. Montgomery by regarding *The Blue Castle* as a parody of romance rather than as a serious attempt at the genre, but I cannot quite convince myself that such is the case.

In the final book which I am to discuss, *Pat of Silver Bush* , the author returns to the female child as protagonist. Pat Gardiner is the fourth of five children. Because her mother is sickly and occupied with a new baby, Pat's upbringing, like that of Anne and Emily, is left to a surrogate parent. Judy Plum is a shanty Irish family retainer whose influence on the "quare child -- touched wid a liddle green rose-thorn " by a leprechaun on the day she was born -- is, from the modern point of view, deplorable. Judy can speak "English" when the Gardiners' fine relatives are present, but in the bosom of the family she affects an Irish brogue in which dialect she fills the child's head with fairy nonsense, assures her that babies are found in parsley beds, passes on malicious gossip, and instills in her a conviction that she is socially superior -- "Remember the Binnies may sweat but the Gardiners perspire". That the lesson has been well learned is evident in a letter that Pat writes to her brother, Sid:

Sylvia Copilla says that Fred Davidson and his sister Muriel used to be devoted to each other just like you and me but they quarreled and now they never speak . . . Of course they are only Davidsons. Sylvia says May Binnie is your girl. She isn't, is she, Sid? You'd never have a Binnie for a girl. They are not in our class.

Pat of Silver Bush contains many of the ingredients found in *Anne* and *Emily* -- the P.E.I. setting, the clan feeling, the visits to eccentric relatives, the bosom friend, the admiring boys, the education at Queen's -- yet when I read *Pat* as a child I found it a disappointment. Pat seems a bore and a snob. Rereading has not changed my mind. Part of Pat's failure to interest us results from the lack of development in her character. Petted by the family and Judy, she is never placed in a position of real crisis where strength of character is required. Moreover, the love of nature which she shares with the other heroines is expressed in such tritely sentimental rhetoric that the character cannot help being diminished. Whether running about in the garden to kiss the flowers or dancing naked under the impression that she is a bewitched princess, she comes across as a girl who is queer to the point of being dim-witted.

Why are Anne and Emily such memorable characters while Valancy and Pat are best forgotten? It is not a question of time bringing to slow fruition a writer's skill, for Anne, the first of Montgomery's creations, is also the best. The answer must be found in the fictional character's relationship to reality. Much of the interest in *Anne* and *Emily* results from the tension between the adults, with their rigid view of how a child should act, and the children, with their strong sense of justice and clear-eyed awareness of adult shortcomings. Though the heroines' characters may have been influenced by such fictional rebels against the establishment as Lewis Carroll's Alice[9] and Mark Twain's Huckleberry Finn, they must also represent the way in which real children reacted to the authoritarian adults who controlled their destinies. Even Kenneth Grahame in that sensitive recreation of happy childhood, *The Golden Age,* inveighs against the Olympians:

> This strange anaemic order of beings was further removed from us, in fact, than the kindly beasts who shared our natural existence. The estrangement was fortified by an abiding sense of injustice, arising from the refusal of the Olympians to defend, to retract, to admit themselves in the wrong, or to accept similar concessions on our part.[10]

When Anne shouts furiously at Mrs. Lynde,

> "How dare you call me skinny and ugly? How dare you say I'm freckled and red-headed? You are a rude, impolite, unfeeling woman!"

she is expressing a justifiable sense of outrage at the insensitivity of adults. And when Emily confronts Aunt Elizabeth with "How dare you touch *my private papers?*" she is asserting her right to be treated as an individual.

Moreover, in *Anne* and *Emily* there is such genuine interaction between children and adults that the adults themselves are changed.

Matthew and Cousin Jimmy, the weak but kindly father figures, are given an interest that lifts them out of the humdrum routine of their daily lives and enables them to stand up to formidable females. Aunt Elizabeth learns that she cannot treat children according to standards that differ from those applied to adults. And Marilla so far overcomes her distrust of emotion that after Matthew's death she confesses her true feelings about Anne:

> I know I've been kind of strict and harsh with you maybe -- but you mustn't think I didn't love you as well as Matthew did, for all that. I want to tell you now when I can. It's never been easy for me to say things out of my heart, but at times like this it's easier. I love you as dear as if you were my own flesh and blood and you've been my joy and comfort ever since you came to Green Gables.

By the same token, what makes Valancy and Pat inadequate is their lack of influence. Valancy's pert put-down of the riddling uncle and boring aunts strikes us as rudeness rather than as a courageous expression of ego, while the self-dramatisation which brings Anne so vividly to life seems, in Valancy, to be maudlin play-acting. There is no better testimony to the adults' immobility in *The Blue Castle* than the fact that, regardless of how queerly Valancy behaves, her mother and Cousin Stickles continue to sit "drearily, grimly knitting. Baffling and inhuman as ever."

In *Pat of Silver Bush* there is no lack of incident -- births, weddings, the departure of a brother, the death of a friend -- but all is surface fussiness. Because the characters fail to interact with one another we remain uninterested. The lachrymose seems the dominant mood but there is no sense of proportion. Tears gush forth as profusely when Father shaves his beard as when the bosom friend dies. At the same time, there is no development of Pat's character. The woman who becomes "the Chatelaine of Silver Bush" is really no different from the seven-year-old listening to Judy's stories.

In the end, what contributes most of all to the sense of reality projected by Anne and Emily is the fact that the fabric of their lives is that of L. M. Montgomery's own experience."[11] Lucy Maud, too, was a motherless child brought up by relatives in a farmhouse at Cavendish, Prince Edward Island. She, too, struck callers as "queer" because she talked to objects, individually named apple trees, and imaginatively created child companions who were "kindred spirits". She suffered from the tension between Puritan expectations and the working of original sin. Years later, she wrote to Weber, "Some of the me's are good, some *not*".[12] Like Anne and Pat, she had to stay at home to care for an elderly, ailing lady rather than embarking on travel or a career:

> You say you wonder why I didn't travel. It is simply because I cannot leave home. Grandma is 82 and I cannot leave her, for even a week's cruise. We live all alone and there is no one I can get to stay with her. I am very much tied down but it cannot be helped.[13]

The most nearly autobiographical of her child characters is Emily Starr. The jet black hair and deep blue eyes, the affection for cats, the stories of Scottish ancestors, the family pride, the strict Calvinistic upbringing, the sensitivity about being different from other children at school, the escape on the wings of imagination and the gift for the written word -- "the best method of soul cultivation there is"[14] -- belong to Lucy Maud. By using the epistolary device -- Emily's letters to her dead father -- the author projects an intimacy of experience that her other books lack:

> There has been a dark shadow over this day. I dropped my cent in church.. It made a dreadful noise. It felt as if everybody looked at me.

> My heart is very sore tonight. Mike died this morning. Cousin Jimmy says he must have been poisoned.

> I think maybe I'll write novels when I grow up as well as poetry. But Aunt Elizabeth won't let me read any novels so how can I find out how to write them?

The success with which Montgomery presents teen-age boys -- Jingles, the only believable character in *Pat,* Perry and Teddy in *Emily,* and Gilbert who achieved immortality when he whispered "Carrots!" -- results from her childhood association with Wellington and Dave who boarded at her Grandmother's, while the vivid pictures of uncles, aunts and cousins testify to the close observation of experienced clan life.

Because the author is so closely identified with Anne and Emily, she is able to present events, settings and other characters as they would be seen through the eyes of children. Anne's exuberant and exaggerated response to Green Gables is acceptable to the reader because it is appropriate to the character. Emily's appreciation of the Murray kitchen is what one might expect from a sharp-eyed eleven-year-old:

> The sanded floor was spotlessly white, but the boards had been scrubbed away through the years until the knots in them stuck up all over in funny little bosses . . . In one corner of the ceiling was a large square hole which looked black and spookish in the candlelight, and made her feel creepy. *Something* might pop down out of a hole like that if one hadn't behaved just right, you know.

In *Pat of Silver Bush* and *The Blue Castle* there is a confusion between the persona of the character and that of the author, with the cliché, cuteness and excessive romanticism which are evident in the author's own letters being imposed on the characters. For example, Valancy's rhapsodizing over the Blue Castle "drowned in sunset lilac light, incredibly delicate and elusive" seems inappropriate language for a thirty-year-old woman, even one who is considered queer.

In a letter of March 2, 1908,[15] Montgomery somewhat deprecatingly describes *Anne* as "a story written more especially for girls and not pretending to be of any intrinsic interest to adults." Whether an author is justified in placing limits of age and sex on a book is a questionable point; even more questionable is the implication that inferior writing is permissible in a book intended for children. That this kind of condescension mars many of L. M. Montgomery's books is unfortunately true. She wrote her "little yarns . . . with an eye single to Sunday School scholars"[16] as she told Weber in the last of the extant Cavendish letters. But Anne, the queer child, was approvingly received by the prestigious adult periodical, the *Spectator*. "I *did* feel flattered."

NOTES

[1] *The Republic of Childhood*, (Toronto, 1967), p. 252.

[2] "The Problem of a Canadian Literature" in *Masks of Fiction,* ed. A.J.M. Smith (Toronto, 1961), p. 41.

[3] Cited in M.M.Mitchell's Foreword to Hilda M. Ridley's *The Story of L. M. Montgomery* (London, 1956). L. M. Montgomery gives another version of Mark Twain's views: "He wrote me that in *Anne* I had created 'the dearest and most lovable child in fiction since the immortal Alice'." See *The Green Gables Letters from L. M. Montgomery to Ephraim Weber 1905-1909*, ed. Wilfrid Eggleston (Toronto, 1960), p. 80.

[4] cf. James Janeway's *A Token for Children: being an Exact Account of the Conversion, Holy and Exemplary Lives, and Joyful Deaths of several Young Children* (c. 1670).

[5] Boswell's *Life of Johnson*, Oxford Standard Authors (London 1953), p. 487.

[6] See Leonard de Vries, ed. *Little Wide-Awake, an Anthology from Victorian Children's Books and Periodicals in the collection of Anne and Fernand G. Renier* (London, 1967); *Young Wilfred or the Punishment of Falsehood* (London, 1821); Frederic Farrar's *Eric, or Little by Little* (London, 1858); and Heinrich Hoffman's *Struwwelpeter* (trans. London, 1848) for examples of the type.

[7] Writing to Weber on September 10, 1908, L. M. Montgomery expressed her own awareness of the problem: "Anne, grown-up, couldn't be made as quaint and unexpected as the child Anne." *The Green Gables Letters*, p. 74.

[8] The germ of Anne was a newspaper clipping about a couple who applied to an orphanage for a boy and were sent a girl instead.

[9] That Montgomery admired Carroll is evident from her allusion to *Through the Looking Glass* in a letter to Weber written on December 16, 1906. See *The Green Gables Letters*, p. 10.

[10] *The Golden Age* (London, 1895), p. 10.

[11] Biographical details are found in Hilda M. Ridley, *The Story of L. M. Montgomery* (London, 1956), and in *The Green Gables Letters,* the General Introduction to which includes a brief autobiography by Montgomery, pp. 5-7.

[12] *The Green Gables Letters,* p. 25.

[13] *Ibid.,* p. 45-56.

[14] *Ibid.,* p. 32.

[15] *Ibid.,* p. 61.

[16] *Ibid.,* pp. 93-94.

Muriel Whitaker teaches Arthurian and Children's Literatures at the University of Alberta. She published an article on the Canadian animal story in the last issue of CCL.

The Land of Lost Content: The Use of Fantasy in L. M. Montgomery's Novels

JANE COWAN FREDEMAN

Into my heart an air that kills
 From yon far country blows:
What are those blue remembered hills,
 What spires, what farms are those?

That is the land of lost content,
 I see it shining plain,
The happy highways where I went
 And cannot come again.

In a passage in *The Story Girl* , L. M. Montgomery elaborates on Housman's description of "the land of lost content," using "fairyland" as a metaphor both for the golden days of childhood and for the font from which creative artists, separated from the common run, continue to draw their imaginative powers:

> "I wish there was such a place as fairyland--and a way to get to it," said Cecily.

> "I think there *is* such a place as fairyland--in spite of Uncle Edward," said the Story Girl dreamily, "and I think there is a way of getting there too, if we could only find it."

Well, the Story Girl was right. There is such a place as fairyland--but only children can find the way to it. And they do not know that it is fairyland until they have grown so old that they forget the way. One bitter day, when they seek it and cannot find it, they realize what they have lost and that is the tragedy of life. On that day the gates of Eden are shut behind them and the age of gold is over. Henceforth they must dwell in the common light of common day. Only a few, who remain children at heart, can ever find that fair, lost path again, and blessed are they above mortals. They, and only they, can bring us tidings from that dear country where once we sojourned and from which we must evermore be exiles. The world calls them its singers and poets and artists and story-tellers; but they are just people who have never forgotten the way to fairyland. (pp. 165-66).

When she set out to write her first novel, Montgomery thought she might have "only a very moderate success . . . . I never dreamed that it would appeal to young and old. I thought girls in their teens might like to read it, that was the only audience I hoped to reach."[1] That she and so many others have been surprised by the breadth of her appeal--her novels remain so popular that of twenty-one only *Emily's Quest* is out of print in this country--is, I think, a measure of the failure of sophisticated readers to identify the universals in the world she created.

L. M. Montgomery was a romantic, in expression as well as thought, as the passage above amply illustrates, but in her description of childhood fancy, she continually keeps the real or adult world close to the surface. In the novels the reader finds not only more or less elaborate descriptions of the heroine's fantasy worlds but also constant, and frequently harsh, intrusions by adults who have lost fairyland and by a tribe of children who have never entered it. The disappointments and griefs, trivial or serious, imaginary or real, which characterize her novels may be seen as milestones on the road to the gateway of adulthood, the time of initiation when all but a privileged few must leave the "Golden Road."

There are dozens of children--"Pilgrims" Montgomery calls them--on this road in the novels, but it is mainly through the heroines--from the little-known Marigold Lesley, Jane Stuart, and Valancy Stirling, through Pat Gardiner and Emily Starr, to the Story Girl, Sara Stanley, and, of course, Anne--that the reader comes to appreciate both fairyland and its loss. Among the many characteristics these heroines and their foils share, the primary one is isolation or solitariness, even when they are apparently surrounded by family and friends. In order to comprehend Montgomery's purpose, the reader must recognize this shared condition; at the same time he must also understand the distinction made in the novels between fantasy and those true glimpses beyond the veil which separate the real from an ideal world. In *The Alpine Path,* Montgomery reveals many of the details of her own fantasies, but she also describes this visionary aspect:

> It has always seemed to me, ever since early childhood, that, amid all the commonplaces of life, I was very near to a kingdom of ideal beauty. Between it and me hung only a thin veil. I could never draw it quite aside, but sometimes a wind fluttered it and I caught a glimpse of the enchanting realm beyond--only a glimpse, but those glimpses have made life worth while.[2]

Like their author, most of the heroines and their playmates either inhabit or create fantasy worlds, but only a few experience what Emily calls "the flash."

Most of the heroines' game-playing can be seen as a process by which they extend and enrich the boundaries of their childhood lives, but for some the fantasy is more completely escapist. Thus, though Valancy Stirling and Marigold Lesley are not typical in their use of the fantasy world, to exclude them from an examination of the theme of fairyland would both lessen the appreciation of Montgomery's reliance on it in her work and suggest, by omission, that she did not recognize this purpose of fantasy. Both characters have in common that they are dominated and patronized by their relations; that their feelings seem never to be taken into consideration; that they are essentially friendless; and that they possess neither the beauty nor the charm and manner which are the saving graces in their real worlds.

Paradoxically, age seems to be irrelevant: Marigold is six when Sylvia appears, while Valancy still occupies her "blue castle" at twenty-nine. On the surface Sylvia parallels those imaginary playmates who are conjured up by almost all solitary children who have to rely on their imaginations, and the reactions of Marigold's mother and grandmother parallel those of most adults. Her weak and colourless mother, perhaps more dominated even than Marigold herself, sees no harm in a fantasy which gives her daughter such pleasure; "young grandmother," however, tries--first by persuasion and then by force--to deny Marigold entrance into the "land where wishes come true" by locking the "Magic Door" through which the child must pass before she can incant her "rhyme" and gain access to Sylvia. Only the intercession of the psychologist, Dr. Adam Clow, prevents Marigold from wasting away when she is deprived of the fantasy that has become life. To the statement that she is living falsehoods, Dr. Clow replies:

> . . . They are truths to her. She sees things invisible to us . . . . She is not trying to deceive anybody. she has the wonderful gift of creation in an unusual degree. It is such a pity that she will lose it as she grows older--that she will have to forego its wonder and live, like us, in the light of common day . . . . (p. 116)[3]

Marigold creates Sylvia because she has no playmates; her rare visits with relatives are not often successful; she is rejected at school; and there are no children living nearby in Harmony. It is only when the last of these conditions alters and she makes friends with Budge Guest that her world begins to change. Marigold has premonitions of this change, and her aunt, one of the rare, sympathetic adults, encourages her to keep her dream, "knowing that since Marigold had begun to think of Sylvia as a dream that the sad awakening is near" (p. 319). Seeking to retain Budge's friendship after a new boy arrives, Marigold foolishly confides to him all the details of Sylvia. She feels disloyal; he regards her fantasy as silly; and Sylvia disappears. But out of her grief, Marigold grows: "The old magic was gone forever--gone with Sylvia and the Hidden Land and all the dear, sweet fading dreams of childhood. But after all there were compensations . . . . She stood on her own ground" (pp. 327-28).

Valancy Stirling, too, learns to stand on her own ground when she exchanges dream for reality. However, given the differences in their ages and the implication that Marigold will have a normal adolescence, Valancy's problems will probably be seen as more serious by the reader. Acquaintance with her odious relatives--the mother whom she is afraid to offend, her uncle Benjamin for whose jokes she is the constant butt, and her beautiful cousin Olive--makes it obvious why she "had lived spiritually in the Blue Castle ever since she could remember . . . . All that supported her through the boredom of her days was the hope of going on a dream spree at night'' (pp. 4-5). But even when the story opens, it is Valancy's "day of fate," and she cannot "find the key of her Blue Castle.'' Thus, hers is not a story of fantasy but of maturation. It is important to recognize that here and throughout Montgomery's novels the reader does not share the solitary dreams. What Marigold and Sylvia laughed about is not revealed, and only the barest outlines of the series of lovers who inhabited Valancy's castle in Spain are sketched in. What is important is the process by which the real world overtakes the imaginary.

Valancy's change is as abrupt as Sylvia's disappearance. From the moment when plain "Doss,'' "twenty-nine, lonely, undesired, ill-favoured,'' learns from Dr. Trent's short note that with her heart condition she will be lucky to live out the year, she feels a curious freedom from her domineering clan. She resents rather than fears death, "not because she had no future but because she had no past" (p. 47). A "colourless nonentity,'' she had never had the "one wholly happy hour'' which would allow her to be willing to die. In the remainder of the novel she sets out to please herself. "I shall never pretend anything again. I've breathed an atmosphere of fibs and pretences and evasions. . . . I may not be able to do much that I want to do but I won't do another thing that I don't . . ." (pp. 54-55). These lines and the situations that follow reveal the frank forthrightness which often puts Montgomery's younger heroines in awkward situations. Valancy's future actions do not involve her in the kinds of troubles caused by Anne's outspokenness to Mrs. Lynde or Emily's to Miss Brownell, but they do bring her freedom and life.

The beginnings of Valancy's rebellion are simple: she hacks to pieces the rosebush given to her for her birthday, which has, symbolically, refused to bloom; she will no longer attend the Anglican church, simply because it is expected of her; and she not only refuses to assume her expected role at the family dinner, but thinks and speaks a series of home truths. While her family is dismayed about the possible social repercussions, they attempt to humour her until she decides to become housekeeper for the town handyman and drunk, Roaring Abel Gay, and to nurse his dying daughter Cissy. In Abel's rough house she finds herself no longer superfluous. Among the things she does as she eases Cissy's last days is to tell her of the Blue Castle. And the frail girl, ostracized because she has had an illegitimate child as much as because of her father's behaviour, tells her "Everyone has a Blue Castle, I think . . . . Only everyone has a different name for it. I had mine--once" (p. 108).

During this time, too, Valancy comes to know the mysterious Barney Snaith, a figure around whom the town has woven lurid tales. In time she recognizes that she loves him and suddenly feels a woman, "justified to herself." After Cissy dies, not wanting to live what she thinks are her last few weeks or months at home, Valancy gives him the doctor's letter and asks him to marry her. When to her surprise he agrees, she goes with him to his island. At her first glimpse of the shack surrounded by pines in the moonlight, she recognizes her blue castle. For a time she lives utterly happy in a world of freedom, "a world where time was not--which was young with immortal youth--where there was neither past nor future but only the present" (p. 179).

But this dream, too, must end. With the series of coincidences, dramas, and revelations which mark her work, Montgomery brings the novel to a happy conclusion. First, Valancy learns she had received the wrong letter and is not in danger of death. Then she discovers that Barney Snaith is both the son of the millionaire supplier of Redfern's patent medicines and the John Foster who authored the nature books she has immersed herself in. Feeling that she has tricked him, Valancy returns home, only, of course, to have Barney, now aware of his own deep feelings, come after her. Finally matured, Valancy is able to leave her second blue castle and enter fully into the real world.

Although the plots of many of the greatest English novelists are full of coincidences and happy endings, Montgomery is frequently condemned for employing these obvious devices. Montgomery believed in a personal "City of Fulfilment" and an incident in her career at the Halifax *Echo*, which she was to elaborate in *Emily's Quest*, reveals how it affected her work. The ending of a serial having been lost, Montgomery was requested to provide one. Years later she saw the original, "about as different from mine as anything could possible be." In the novel the original author arrives at Emily's door in a rage to tell her, "My story was barbarously mutilated. A happy ending. Horrible. *My* ending was sorrowful and artistic. A happy ending can never be artistic" (p. 183). L. M. Montgomery did not agree, any more than did Dickens, who transformed *Great Expectations* into a totally different work by the substitution of the second, happy ending.

For all their differences, Valancy and Marigold illustrate the primary theme of Montgomery's work, the encroachment of the real world on the child and the need to leave childhood behind. Only two, the Story Girl and Emily Starr, will not become exiles from fairyland, though for all a contented future is envisioned. Her heroines share further common traits which serve to accentuate their solitude.

Perhaps to mark the individuality of growth and perhaps because it echoed her own experience, with the exception of Pat Gardiner all Montgomery's heroines are isolated from the normal pattern of family life. Marigold and Valancy have only one living parent, and neither mother is able or willing to help her child. Jane Stuart believes her situation to be the same until she learns that her parents are separated. Anne, Emily, and Kilmeny are orphans living with elderly people who cannot, even when they try, comprehend their private worlds. The Story Girl whose mother is dead and whose father is abroad, is a further variation; her home is with an aunt and uncle, near, but not with, her numerous cousins.

Many minor characters share this particular difference from their peers, and the reader is frequently invited to enlarge upon their fantasies as well. In *The Story Girl* for example, the hired boy, Peter, is an orphan, while Beverley and Felix King and the mournful Sara Ray all have only one living parent. Jane Stuart's Toronto friend, Jody, is an orphan. Ilse Burnley and Teddy Kent have only single parents, both embittered by the way in which they lost their mates, and the fourth of the New Moon group, Perry Miller, is an orphan from Stovepipe Town. In this group the other dream worlds are more clear. Ilse is to be an elocutionist (a story-teller); Teddy, an artist, and Perry, a lawyer and politician. Even Pat Gardiner's friend, Hilary Gordon, has been deserted by his mother and is kept by his aunt and uncle in the spirit of "duty" which sheds such dark clouds over these young lives. To this list could be added, among others, Gay Penhallow, Brian Dark, and a number of other characters from *A Tangled Web*, but each of their stories is only a small part of that complex plot.

The heroines also tend to be isolated or differentiated from the other girls in the books by their plainness and by the oddity of their clothes, aspects almost as frequently commented upon as the gratitude expected from them by their surrogate and real parents. The truism that beauty is only skin deep is documented dramatically in Montgomery's novels where internal rather than external beauty is a prerequisite for the final emergence of the character; frequently too, it separates those other characters who recognize the depth and uniqueness of the heroines' visions and dreams from those who are incapable of doing so. Though all recognize that they are "nae beauties," Anne seems more keenly self-conscious about her carrot hair and freckles, and in none of the other novels are the episodes involving the recognition of plainness so hilarious as the hair-dying scene in *Anne of Green Gables*. The burden falls lightest on Marigold and Pat; neither are jealous children, and the former's most earnest hope is to have her hair bobbed, while Pat learns at eleven that her eyes, her smile, and her capacity for love will carry her further then any amount of golden curls. Emily's good points are like Pat's, though she inwardly rages, like Anne, at her old-fashioned clothes and earnestly wants the "band" she feels will make her prettier. The Story Girl's too long and too white face is more than compensated for by the rainbow voice which in the future, the reader is told, will make kings delight to honour her. The boyish Beverly King wonders how it is that she cast the beautiful Felicity in the shade:

> I looked at her and wondered why it was not enough that she should be so pretty and capable of making such turnovers. If only she were more interesting! Felicity had not a particle of the nameless charm and allurement which hung about every motion of the Story Girl, and made itself manifest in her lightest word and most careless glance. (p. 40)

Beverly is, of course, narrating in retrospect, but throughout the two novels, the effects of the Story Girl on children and adults alike are manifest.

The naming of places, trees, and objects is another personal trait which Montgomery transfers to her heroines. Whether or not these secret names are shared with others, it is the meaning the heroine invests them with that makes them live. Thus, for example, Diana

Barry, though she wants to share Anne's games, lacks the depth of Anne's feelings to actualize for herself the "Lake of Shining Waters," "White Way of Delight," and "Dryad's Bubble," among others. So, too, all of the children and adults in *The Story Girl* know the names of the trees in the old orchard, but only she can revivify the long gone people for whom they were named and create the sensation Beverley says the children could feel but were unable to analyze. The orchard was different because "it blossomed not only apple blossoms but all the love, faith, joy, pure happiness, and pure sorrow of those who had made it and walked there"(p. 56).

The betrayal or outgrowing of these childhood names often separates the heroine from her peers. Just as Budge thought Sylvia "silly," so there comes a day when Pat's beloved brother Sid turns his back on their "Secret Field" by showing it to May Binnie to whom it is only "a hole in the woods." For Pat, May is the equivalent of Anne's Josie Pye, and through her and the many other stodgy, unimaginative, or cruel children, L. M. Montgomery introduces a view of childhood which contradicts the assumption that all children are inhabitants of fairyland. The view is more akin to the one expressed in e. e. cumming's lyric "anyone lived in a pretty how town." There only the children--and not all of them--can recognize the love between anyone and no one:

> children guessed (but only a few
> and down they forgot as up they grew
> ....
> and only the snow can begin to explain
> how children are apt to forget to remember

Sid was one of the few, but "down he forgot" by the time he married May. Pat's story illustrates another use of emblematic names. Throughout both books her home, "Silver Bush," represents everything to Pat. She thinks she is free and happy to have it alone when she finally decides not to marry David Kirk, but after Rae's departure and Judy's death, there are signs that for Pat, too, things must change. Alone, she decides to light up the house:

> It did not like to be dark and silent. Yet she paused for a moment on the door-step, the prey of a sudden fancy. That shut door was a door of dreams through which she might slip into the Silver Bush of long ago . ... . A world utterly passed away might be her universe. (p. 328)

Pat knows the fancy is "nonsense," but it cannot be dissipated until the emblem is gone. Her dreams go through fire as Silver Bush burns: "nothing was left . . . her heart was like an unlighted room and nothing, *she thought she knew,* could ever illumine it again" (p. 331, italics added). Silver Bush and her devotion to it were not her life but her protection against it, as she finally recognizes when Hilary Gordon, who has not forgotten to remember, comes to her among the ashes to tell her that he has built her a new home by another sea.

Most of the other novels and short stories can be explicated more satisfactorily if this aspect of the characters and plot is given the attention it deserves. There has as yet appeared little criticism of *The Road to Yesterday*. In her review of the book in *Canadian Literature,* Frances Frazer incisively identifies the strengths and weaknesses of L. M. Montgomery's fiction. "Deft characterization," "effectively specific, tart dialogue," and "tough humorous realism" are indeed counter-balanced by "constant wish-fulfilments," "just and beautiful endings,"and "sugared romanticism." [4] However, if the stories are read, as they all can be, as illustrations of the conflict between fantasy and reality, the endings cannot be dismissed as "individually delightful but cumulatively rather sickening." Instead, they are illustrations of how fantasy perpetuated can sour a life for an adult who will not let it go--"A Dream Come True" and "The Reconciliation"--or preserve it for a child who needs it--"An Afternoon with Mr. Jenkins" and "The Cheated Child." Indeed, the late awakening from fantasy can be a happy event for more than one character, as in "Penelope Struts Her Theories," "The Pot and the Kettle," and "Here Comes the Bride."

One character above all others illustrates and summarizes the workings of fantasy in Montgomery's novels--Emily Starr, whose story is told in a trilogy in many ways superior to the far longer Anne series. Though L. M. Montgomery was and still is identified with Anne, any reader of *The Alpine Path* will recognize at once that Emily's biography, appearance, and career more nearly parallel her own. Despite superficial similarities, however, it is dangerous to press character analogues in the novels too closely. Montgomery would have endorsed wholeheartedly Thomas Wolfe's disclaimer in the proem to *Look Homeward Angel* that whereas "all serious work in fiction is autobiographical . . . fiction is not fact," and "a novelist may turn over half the people in a town to make a single figure in his novel." Like Wolfe, Montgomery meditated no man's or girl's--especially not her own--portrait in her books, as she makes plain in *The Alpine Path*: "Now for my own part, I have never, during all the years I have studied human nature, met one human being who could, as a whole, be put into a book without injuring it." [5] She is to be included in this stricture, and those incidents in Emily's life which do or do not accord with her own are therefore not noted.

The eight-year-old Emily to whom the reader is introduced in *Emily of New Moon* has all the accoutrements of a full-blown child of fantasy. For companions she has the Wind Woman, Emily-in-the-glass, and various trees. But above all she has her writing, through which she can record her joys and dissipate her sorrows, and "the flash."

> It couldn't be described--not even to Father, who always seemed a little puzzled by it. Emily never spoke of it to anyone else. It had always seemed to Emily, ever since she could remember, that she was very, very near to a world of wonderful beauty. Between it and herself hung only a thin curtain; she could never draw the curtain aside--but sometimes, just for a moment, a wing fluttered it and then it was as if she caught a glimpse of the enchanting realm beyond--only a glimpse--and

67

heard a note of unearthly music.

> This moment came rarely--went swiftly, leaving her breathless with the inexpressible delight of it. She could never recall it--never summon it--never pretend it; but the wonder of it stayed with her for days . . . . (p. 7)

At her father's death, Emily is turned over to her mother's reluctant family, who eventually draw lots to decide who must take her. The first impressions Emily makes on them are even more unpropitious than Anne's on Marilla. But from the moment when "the flash" returns and with it "courage and hope" for "her cold little soul," Emily never falters in her sense of justice or in her forthrightness. When her Aunt Elizabeth demands to see the account book in which she keeps her writings, she burns it; when her father is called a failure, she retaliates. So, too, as she settles into New Moon, she learns she can master both the children--who reject her "because you ain't a bit like us"--and even her aunt Elizabeth, when "some formidable power in [her] soul" brings Archibald Murray's expression to her face.

After various minor disappointments, she is soon friends with Ilse, Teddy, and Perry, and the characteristics of the fantasy worlds of Montgomery's other heroines begin to become part of the way in which she enlarges her solitary imaginings. Names are provided in abundance for their haunts, the most important among them for the future being "The Disappointed House" and the Roads of Today, Yesterday, and Tomorrow. Play-acting, though frowned upon, flourishes, and she has repeated clashes with her first teacher and her aunt over her writing, particularly of "untrue" things, as time passes. But these reactions are compensated for by her relationships with such adults as Aunt Laura, who sympathizes without understanding, "queer" Cousin Jimmy, who soom becomes the provider of the Jimmy books in which her fancies take form, and Mr. Carpenter, who recognizes her talent and savagely corrects her writing.

Above all there is Dean "Jarback" Priest, a college friend of her father's, who, perceiving an inner beauty which he describes as "prismatic--palpitating--elusive," calls her, poetically, Star. Their special relationship builds through the years. To Emily "Dean Priest was sealed of her tribe and she divined it instantly. He had a right to the inner sanctuary and she yielded it unquestioningly" (p. 279). For Dean, a different fantasy takes form: he "became a boy again with a boy's untainted vision," and he dreams of possessing his Star.

Dean Priest is probably the most difficult of L. M. Montgomery's characters to comprehend. The reader is not normally shown so much of the character of any of the heroines' lovers and is, consequently, not so torn when a choice between them comes. Perhaps Montgomery intended him as a figure to replace the equally sensitive Douglas Starr in Emily's life, for in certain ways he can be compared to the fathers her other heroines regain--the bohemian Blair Stanley, dissipating his talents and energies as he tells fascinating stories of his wanderings around the world; and the stronger Andrew Stuart who encourages his child to grow as she will. However, despite his external deformity, the inner "strength and tenderness and humour"--with which Montgomery inbues Dean from the outset and which he constantly demonstrates--makes him equally suitable as lover.

In *Emily of New Moon* , Dean defines fairyland as "everything the heart desires." In *Emily's Quest* he has to lose his fantasy, though he comes close to having it in his grasp. Perhaps Dean is voicing Montgomery's feeling when he says at the time their engagement is broken, "I should have known that only youth can call to youth--and I was never young. If I ever had been, even though I am old now, I might have held you"(p. 128). But this explanation is not satisfactory; it could have been said to Pat by David Kirk. Dean's jealousy of Emily's work and his criticism of it, which led her to burn her first novel, provocatively entitled *A Seller of Dreams*, is perhaps intended to show more truly why he could never capture and hold her as Teddy Kent can.

Though the relationship between Emily and Teddy is not as fully developed as that with Dean, the reader is not unprepared for Emily's realization that she loves Teddy. Throughout their years apart, sufficient reminders of the days when they dreamed of sharing "The Disappointed House," when Emily always responded to Teddy's whistle, and when they vowed always to think of one another at the sight of Vega of the Lyre, are given to keep Teddy in mind, as do the intermittent references to the way in which Emily's eyes and smile continue to inform his paintings from his earliest days until he is recognized as an artist.

Emily's awareness of the totality of their bond comes as a result of one trait, occasionally implied in other heroines, but defined only in Emily. Closely connected with "the flash," but coming to her in dream or illness instead of waking hours, are moments of prescience. Through some kind of vision the child Emily had discovered the mystery of Ilse's mother's disappearance; in adolescence, she divines the location of a lost child; and, finally, calling to him through space, drawing "aside the veil of sense and time and see[ing] beyond," Emily saves Teddy from sailing on the *Flavian*. These moments are frightening and ennervating for Emily, but through them

> She *knew*, beyond any doubt or cavil or mockery, that she had seen Teddy--had saved,   or tried to   save him, from some unknown peril. And she knew, just as simply and just as surely that she loved him--had always loved him, with a love that lay at the very foundation of her being. (pp. 120-21)

Anne may be, in Bliss Carman's words, "one of the immortal children of fiction," and so she certainly has been for several generations of L. M. Montgomery's readers. But it is Emily who fully encompasses the complex fantasy worlds which Montgomery shaped in her novels.

NOTES

[1] L. M. Montgomery, *The Alpine Path* (Don Mills; Fitzhenry and

Whiteside, 1974), p. 76.

2*Ibid*., pp. 47-48.

3Editions cited in this article are *Magic for Marigold* (McClelland and Stewart, 1929), *The Blue Castle* (McClelland and Stewart, 1926), *The Story Girl* (Ryerson, 1944), *Mistress Pat* (McClelland and Stewart, 1925), and *Emily's Quest* (McClelland and Stewart, 1927).

4F. Frazer, "Scarcely an End," *Canadian Literature* 63 (Winter 1975), 90-91. The publisher has done the author a disservice in a prefatory statement that the stories seem to be placed in "the immediate pre-World War II period," when in fact they can, with the exception of the last, clearly be dated to the days of *Rainbow Valley* and *Rilla of Ingleside* by the ages of the Blythe children mentioned. Walter's death at Courcellette (1917) is mentioned as a thing of the past in one story, and "The Road to Yesterday" is obviously in the twenties, but the rest are clearly pre-World War I or immediately after it.

5 *The Alpine Path* p. 72.

Jane Cowan Fredeman is Editor of the University of British Columbia Press.

But What About Jane?

JEAN LITTLE

Lucy Maud Montgomery was directly responsible for a heinous crime I committed when I was ten. Grandma was reading *Anne of Ingleside* aloud. Young Walter Blythe had just walked "all the way from Lowbridge" because a child there had told him that his mother was sick, probably dying. When Walter, after a nightmare journey, finally reached home, he found the house in darkness. Anne was obviously dead. And there the chapter ended.

"Go ON, Grandma!" we begged.

Grandma, serenely aware that Anne could not succumb with so much of that book and a couple of sequels yet to go, refused, put down the closed book on the dresser, said good-night and left. As much an abject slave to my imagination as Walter was to his, I could not bear it. The moment it was safe, I took the book to the window through which moonlight helpfully poured, found the place with trembling hands and READ AHEAD! Anne lived!! Back in bed, I felt miraculously freed of dread for a few moments. Then an awareness of my horrendous wrongdoing oppressed me. Nobody ever read ahead. The next day, I went about haunted by the conviction that the instant Grandma picked up the book, she would somehow guess my full guilt. When, with no word or look of accusation, she calmly launched into Chapter 10, my relief was so evident that she apologized for not reading more the night before. I knew I should confess; I said not a word. I did not tell until I was safely a grown-up myself. But I did not forget what I had done or why or how it all felt.

Montgomery also remembered exactly how it was to be a child. More than that, she was able to record the experience of being a child so faithfully and vividly that reading children, years later, find themselves in her stories. These two linked gifts, first the almost total recall and second the craft which enabled her to use this rich material, are what keep L. M. Montgomery alive. Her writing is flawed. She is overly sentimental and whimsical, although these qualities were welcome in children's fiction at the time when she wrote her books. She has an irritating preoccupation with matchmaking. She revels in describing whole clans of eccentric relations who have little or nothing to do with the plot. As a matter of fact, she seems to find it extremely difficult to leave any place, person or thing without giving it a full description. She frequently loses control of her "minor" characters. In *Pat of Silver Bush,* for example, the heroine is thoroughly upstaged by the family servant

71

who gets to say at least fifty words to Pat's one. Montgomery's sense of humour saves her time and time again but also deserts her sometimes when she is badly in need of it. All of these weaknesses and more are to be found in Montgomery's many, many pages. Yet they are cancelled out to a great extent by the fact that Lucy Maud Montgomery knows about children.

She understands exactly what humiliates a child and how that child responds to it. She knows the way a child's conscience will magnify a small misdeed into a Sin of major proportions, a torment to be wrestled with in the darkness. The terrors children suffer in her books are gargantuan and usually the child perceives them as something that will pursue him forever. Montgomery is always aware that, for her heroes and heroines, the present is all that has actuality. She knows, too, the fatal ease and rapidity with which an adventure can become a disaster and how powerless and angry a child feels as adults manipulate his life without thought of consulting him. That sounds like enough but there is so much more this author understands. How confusing it is for children to be well-behaved in a world where the rules keep changing! How bitterly a child can resent casual well-meant teasing! And how sweet, how passing sweet, are the moments of victory, revenge, and eventual understanding! In *Emily of New Moon,* the child Emily Starr writes:

> A good many things I don't understand but I will remember them and find out about them someday.

This vow each of us made and, later, kept. But how many of us would remember without writers with Montgomery's perceptive memory to remind us?

As I have already indicated, much of L. M. Montgomery's awareness reaches us through mediocre writing. I could devote the rest of this article to outlining the limitations of her talent as a creative writer and as an objective editor and rewriter of her own work, giving chapter and verse as proof. I would find this a pointless exercise. Given these limitations, plus the handicap of writing in a time when sentimentality was not only accepted but immensely popular, Montgomery still did achieve something memorable. What was it?

Or would the question be better put Who were they?

Anne Shirley is, of course, Montgomery's famous heroine. Whether or not you personally like, love or loathe Anne, I think it is safe to say that she will outlive anybody now reading this article. Recently I lived in Japan for a couple of years. Whenever I said I was a Canadian, a Japanese would invariably respond with obvious excitement, "Are you from Prince Edward Island? Do you know Anne of the red hair?" More than one schoolgirl or young woman told me, in deep seriousness, "It is my life's dream to go to Canada and see this Prince Edward Island." I have tried asking children, so far only Canadian children, "Have you read the Anne books?" One would claim to have read the entire series eleven or so times, another to have given up after the first chapter of *Anne of Green Gables* . Not a child looked blank and asked "What Anne books?" Then I tried "Have you read the Emily books?" Granted there are not so many of them. Still, instant recognition on the part of children just was not there. Yet, in spite of Anne's popularity or perhaps because of it, I plan to ignore her, as much as possible, for the remainder of this article. I was devoted to her once and I have not lost my fondness for her during her harumscarum childhood, though I find her less engaging as she matures. But she was never my favourite among Montgomery's heroines. Jane was, in *Jane of Lantern Hill,* And, after rereading masses of Montgomery, I find I remain partial to Jane.

I want, therefore, to look more closely at Jane and at some of the other children Montgomery created, for I believe it was the children who kept us reading all those books, except for the one small space in time when we were twelve or so and became captivated by *The Blue Castle.*

This one lapse is easily understood by those of us who remember ourselves as reading twelve-year-olds. The book is purely and simply a dream, more literate and enchanting than those found in Love Comics. When dreaming is the biggest part of life, *The Blue Castle* is more than satisfactory. The current booming sales of Harlequin Romances and their ilk show that many people do not grow beyond the need for the fantasy world in *The Blue Castle* . Montgomery's effort is much better than some, which is not to heap praises upon her head but merely to give her her due. She at least spices it with humour.

Often, throughout all her books, Lucy Maud Montgomery's sense of the ridiculous or her abrupt return to the mundane saves her from banality. Also her wit is delightful when she does not exploit it. This bit, from *Magic for Marigold* , is one illustration chosen from among hundreds.

> Gwennie stuck out her tongue at Grandmother. It gave Marigold a shock to realize that anybody could do that and live.

To return to the children! Not every child coming from Montgomery's busy pen does her credit. She seems, to me, to have written about four types of children: Stock Children, Non-Children, Exaggerated Children and Real Children. These classifications are not as neat and airtight as I make them sound because Montgomery occasionally loses track of what kind of child she has in hand and lets him or her slip momentarily into being somebody else. This does not trouble child readers unduly since they too step out of character every so often. Critical adults accept such lapses with less equanimity.

The best illustrations of Stock Children are to be found in *The Story Girl* and its sequel *The Golden Road.* Since these two books are in no way separate stories, I shall discuss them as one. Eight children are involved and every one is what I call a Stock Child. Each is early given certain identifying characteristics which never vary. Felix is fat and sensitive about it. Felicity, more complex, is pretty, vain, a good cook, and a snob. She is also always jealous of her cousin Sara and at odds with her brother Dan. Dan is sarcastic. (I read this story carefully less than two months ago and I honestly cannot remember another thing about Dan.) Cecily, sister to Dan and Felicity, is almost a carbon copy of

Beth in *Little Women* (although Beth will be remembered long after Cecily is forgotten). Cecily is good, gentle, timidly brave, and patient throughout. We are given to understand, after making our way through seven-hundred-and-nineteen pages, that dear Cecily will not live to grow up and we feel not the slightest twinge of shock at the news. Peter, the hired boy, is lively, irreverent, and smitten with Felicity. (When Montgomery writes about hired boys, she makes it crystal clear that they are not made of the same stuff as The Family, but she gives them gumption and intelligence and hints, if she does not spell it out, that they will rise in the world and make their mark. An interesting essay could be written on her whole treatment of class distinctions. Anne, for instance, although definitely an orphan. is discovered to have sprung from genteel stock. By their relatives shall ye know them.) Sara Ray, a neighbour child, cries. Always! Sara Stanley, the fabled Story Girl herself, is a heroine who is not a heroine because Montgomery never gives her a plot within which she can develop into a real person. She remains another Stock Child, although the most complicated. She is always vivid, mysterious, charming, slightly humanized by her inability to learn to cook, and so ever ready with a story that I, for one, sometimes longed to tape her mouth shut. Beverley, the narrator of the whole thing, is pompous and ordinary. He also, for a very good reason, sounds middle-aged.

In *The Alpine Path* Lucy Maud Montgomery declares:

> *The Story Girl. . . .* is my own favourite among my books, the one that gave me the greatest pleasure to write, the one whose characters and landscape seem to me most real.₁

When she wrote this, she had not reached the end of her career as a writer, but she had had seven novels published. Why, one wonders, was she so partial to this early effort? I suspect the reason lies, in part at least, in the fact that the book took so little effort to write. She did not have to struggle with plot or search for ways to reveal change and growth in her characters. There is no sustained plot and nobody changes. At the same time, through the handy vehicle of the babbling Story Girl, Montgomery was able to relish retelling all the family and local legends to which she had listened with fascination during her own childhood. And she provided herself, alias the Story Girl, with a highly satisfactory audience, always ready to drop everything and listen spellbound. She failed to realize that a story told has an immediacy which is missing in that same story written down, unless the writer is someone with a storytelling gift far exceeding Montgomery's. It is only fair to say that few and far between are the writers who can successfully interject the telling of a tale which is not vitally linked to the plot of the characters. It has been tried, time and again, by the ablest of authors, and it has been my observation that children invariably simply skip to where "the real story" picks up again.

The Story Girl-Golden Road succeeds seldom, but that is not due simply to the fact that the children are Stock Children. Such boys and girls are the heroes and heroines of many excellent books. Arthur Ransome's characters, to a much lesser extent than Montgomery's, are

74

Stock Children much of the time. John and Susan are consistently dependable and in charge, Nancy always up to deviltry, Peggy a born follower, and so on. But so much happens in his books and his writing draws you on with its magic so skilfully that you do not notice, mind, or even believe that the children remain static in character. Montgomery, also, can make her Stock Children come alive. Before I reread the books, I found I remembered only one incident clearly, but I did remember one and at least thirty years had passed since I had read the story. It was the time when the children learned that the coming of the end of the world had been prophesied and the date had been printed in the newspaper! The group grew more and more terrified as the fateful hour approached. I shared their terror. What child has not spent uneasy minutes pondering over this eventuality? The children in the book plagued adults with questions which sought reassurance but brought upon them nothing save amusement and teasing. I found I still recalled their solemn vows to reform their entire lives if only the world be permitted to remain as always. I felt with them intense relief, joy, and freedom when the hour passed and the Last Trumpet had not sounded. Why did I recollect this when every single story Sara Stanley told had vanished from my memory leaving no trace? It was not because the eight acted unpredictably; it was because they acted. Something dramatic was actually happening instead of being recounted. We read other L. M. Montgomery books till they were in tatters; we left these two looking almost as untouched as the day they were purchased.

The author made two other major mistakes with this book. The worst was that the entire story is told in retrospect by an adult forty years or so after the action, what there was of it, took place. Yesterday is not the world children inhabit, not unless an artist can, like Hester Burton or Geoffrey Trease, turn "the olden days" into now. Sentences like the following, which comes fairly early in *The Story Girl,* destroy the reader's feeling of being himself right in the thick of things.

> Never had I heard a voice like hers. Never, in all my life since, have I heard such a voice.

Compulsive readers or devoted Montgomery fans will keep going. The others, and there are far more of them, will drop the book and look for something offering more involvement.

Montgomery also gave in to the temptation to help fill up her manuscript by including examples of writing ostensibly done by her child characters. This is fun for an author to do. Do you really know your characters so well and do you have the skill necessary to do their writing for them, allowing each his or her individual style? Style or idiosyncrasy? Many authors, often unconsciously I would guess, end up with one eye on their adult audience who will enjoy grammatical absurdities, flowery or wildly inappropriate descriptions, and hilarious spelling errors. I remember shrinking inside as my grandmother laughed heartily over these parodies. "Do they laugh like that at the things I show them, when I'm not there?" a sensitive child asks. The answer is clearly "Yes".

I must make clear, before leaving this point, that there are times when a child's writing forms an integral part of the book itself. Emily Starr, in *Emily of New Moon* is a child in the first apprenticeship stages of becoming a writer. She has to fight her formidable Aunt Elizabeth for her right to keep what amounts to a journal and to keep what she writes in it private. From her schoolmates, she wins both praise and mockery for her efforts. She suffers cruel ridicule from one teacher and, later, accepts severe yet encouraging criticism from another about her writing. The reader needs evidence of Emily's ability or lack of it to make all this plausible. Also Montgomery uses Emily's writing to reveal something of her inner longings, aloneness, resolution, despairs, and so on. Still, Emily's outpourings, while often delightful, should have been cut in half, I think, for here again Montgomery falls back on Emily's telling about things happening instead of letting the reader be there at the very instant. A different sort of example of a child's writing being important to a book is Faith Meredith's open letter to her father's congregation in *Rainbow Valley*. Instead of slowing the plot, this frank epistle sends it forward with alacrity.

The Non-Children, among whom neither Faith nor Emily belong, are hardly worth commenting upon since no child believes in them for an instant. Little Elizabeth, in *Anne of Windy Poplars*, is one. Paul Irving is another. There are others sprinkled here and there. Montgomery fails to give them life. They have not one redeeming flaw. They are always small for their age and they have huge wistful eyes with long lashes and they make impossible speeches:

"You are the only person who loves me in the whole world," said Elizabeth. "When you talk to me I smell violets."

Words like that, issuing from the mouth of a supposed child, made me cringe even when I was a child, and a most uncritical child, myself. I doubt that Montgomery herself was excessively fond of these creatures. They seem to be the type of child appearing least often in her books, and almost never in her best. The Stock Children have fun; the Non-Children may have heard of it but certainly never take part in any.

The Exaggerated Children, on the other hand, usually know far more about fun than is needful. *Magic for Marigold* has two such in rapid succession, Princess Varvara and Marigold's cousin Gwendolen. They are wild, almost amoral children. They are diabolical and outrageous. They are occasionally repentant for the moment or two, but this is never convincing and does not last. Children read about them with awe-struck delight. They are so impossibly wicked and yet they often escape unscathed. But these Exaggerated Children are so busy being bad that they have no time left in which to think or feel, respond or question. The shocks come at one with the staccato quality of the Sesame Street commercials. To have number facts presented in rapid fire succession is one thing; to be so introduced to a person is another. It may leave the reader gasping with a combination of horror and pleasure, but it also leaves him definitely on the outside, looking on. On the other hand, all children have exaggerated days or wish they dared, so these "holy terrors" of Montgomery's have their place.

"But what about Jane?" a voice demands with pardonable impatience.

Jane is one of the Real Children. Yet among the Real Children there are futher divisions. There are the inferior Real Children, those lacking in Imagination but strong on faithfulness like Diana Barry in *Anne of Green Gables* or those who begin as irritating prigs but become people like Cousin Phyllis in *Jane of Lantern Hill*. And there are the superior Real Children who experience "The Flash" like Emily Starr or have Imagination like Anne Shirley. These superior beings, the ones who really matter, usually talk a blue streak, often astonish and/or shock their elders with their precocity, suffer agonies--but believable ones which the reader suffers with them--are humiliated, misunderstood and misjudged, but come out victorious over all in the end. They are totally alive, exceedingly human, and yet possess an added something. Could it be that this plus factor, whatever it may be, removes them just slightly from the rest of us? Are they, maybe, every so often, too wonderful?

Saying so is heresy because we love them, Anne and Emily at least. Marigold might have fared better if she had been allowed into the story before page forty. Pat, in *Pat of Silver Bush* , was, as far as I was concerned, close to being a Non-Child. I could not understand her stifling fear of change. It seemed not only excessive but silly. So what if her father shaved off his moustache! As a niece of mine, an ardent Montgomery fan, succinctly put it, "Pat's really quite dumb." That this feeling of dread stemmed from real emotion Montgomery herself vividly remembered feeling is a matter of record, but most children's only memory of their mother is not the sight of her lying in her coffin. [2] There can be little doubt that the child Lucy Maud was had more reason to be apprehensive about life than most.

Emily and Anne, however, remain strong heroines, not allowing themselves to be overshadowed or pushed aside by other characters. Ilse Burnley, Emily's friend, is a girl who is both Exaggerated and Real, fiery, unpredictable and interesting, but she never usurps Emily's position as central figure. These Real Children change. They get into trouble and learn how to get out again. They suffer consequences and experience both deep joy and sorrow. They are all heroines should be, if only they were not quite so . . . super-sensitive?

And now, Jane! Jane is the heroine of L. M. Montgomery's last novel and Jane was not met with quite the acclaim her predecessors had won.[3] Why not? Nobody seems to have wondered. Could it be simply that people were startled to encounter a child who was just a child?

I do not for one moment claim that *Jane of Lantern Hill* is a book without flaws. Jane's parents are two of the most far-fetched creatures Montgomery ever concocted. Mother is so fluttery and ineffectual that one longs to swat her. Jane's loyalty to her surprises the reader and even Jane has her moments of doubt. Dad is easier to take because he is cast as the hero with Jane as his heroine. His problem is that he is far too good to be true. He is always ready to spend time with his beloved daughter (even though his love is a trifle late in manifesting itself; for years, Jane does not know she has a father), so handsome that Jane, still unaware of his identity, cuts his picture out of a magazine and fantasizes over it, and so willing to go along with Jane's least whim that it is a good thing for all concerned that Jane is a child with sense. Dad is given only one character defect, and one feels that Montgomery hated to mar him even this much and only did so because it was necessary to the plot. He has a blind faith in and fondness for his sister who, with Jane's maternal grandmother's help, managed to wreck Mother and Dad's marriage before Jane was old enough to set things straight. As I reread the book, I found Mother and Dad as foolish as ever and concluded that Jane was going to have uphill work holding the marriage, mended at the book's happy ending, together.

As I earlier indicated, however, I believe the children, not the adults in Montgomery's books, were what held us. The story of Jane, pitted against adult forces she does not understand, being undermined and nearly destroyed as an independent person by a grandmother who is all the wicked witches and selfish stepmothers rolled into one, and yet somehow managing to keep fighting for her selfhood, still found me involved. I was delighted all over again when, with some help but largely through her own tenacity and maturation, Jane wins through to becoming a person with whom others must reckon.

Jane is described in a few sentences early in the book:

> . . . Jane was not very good at games. She always felt awkward in them. At eleven she was as tall as most girls of thirteen. She towered among the girls of her class. They did not like it and it made Jane feel that she fitted in nowhere.

Does this sound like the same writer who, years before, wrote of Anne Shirley:

> Her face was small and white and thin, also much freckled; her mouth was large and so were her eyes, that looked green in some lights and gray in others.

> . . . an extraordinary observer might have seen that the chin was very pointed and pronounced; that the big eyes were full of spirit and vivacity; that the mouth was sweet-lipped and expressive; that the forehead was broad and full; in short . . . that no commonplace soul inhabited the body of this stray woman-child . . .

Or who wrote concerning Emily Starr:

> She put the faded blue hood on over her long, heavy braid of glossy, jet-black hair, and smiled...The smile began at the corners of her lips and spread over her face in a slow, subtle, very wonderful way...In all else...she was like the Starrs--in her large purplish-grey eyes with their very long lashes and black brows, in her high, white forehead...in the delicate moulding of her pale oval face and sensitive mouth, in the little ears that

78

were pointed just a wee bit to show that she was kin to tribes of elfland.

Whom do most eleven-year-old girls see when they look in their mirrors? Anne? Emily? I saw Jane.

The theme of *Jane of Lantern Hill* is similar to that of the other two, *Anne of Green Gables* and *Emily of New Moon*. At the beginning, the child is found unacceptable as she stands and the adults, or most of them, try to kill, figuratively, the unacceptable person and create another made their liking. All three girls resist. All have allies: Anne in Matthew, Emily in Cousin Jimmy and Aunt Laura, Jane in her father. But the outcomes or solutions differ. Anne and Emily eventually win love for their true selves from those who earlier sought to reshape them, and the two girls, without conscious effort, succeed in softening the harshness and implacability of Marilla and Aunt Elizabeth. As the children gain in power, the adults lose. Jane wins no love from her antagonists nor does she want to, since they are essentially evil rather than merely old-fashioned and strong-willed. Instead Jane becomes strong enough to be herself in spite of them. As she gains self-confidence, her grandmother and her Aunt Irene lose much of their power to hurt her but they are, in no way, redeemed, nor are they reconciled to her as Jane. She is still unacceptable at the end of the book, but their acceptance has become of no importance to her. She has outgrown them.

Jane's position at the outset of the book is shown clearly in the names by which she is called. Jane was christened Jane Victoria, the names of her two grandmothers. Grandmother, who longs to be rid of Jane, calls her Victoria which is her own name. She gives a great deal of herself in an effort to obliterate anything in Jane which suggests that Jane was fathered as well as mothered. Her mother, who loves her child but cannot stand up to her own mother's corroding possessiveness, calls her Jane Victoria. Her father and Jane herself, both of whom want her to be the person she really is, call her Jane. Montgomery's feeling for the importance of names to children is interesting. Anne's insistence that her name be spelled with an 'e' is now famous. Also every book with a strong heroine in it has her name in the title.

Ways of attacking and diminishing a child's sense of her own worth have not changed. The following scene demonstrates this and also shows Montgomery at her best:

> "Tut, tut," said Uncle William, "Victoria could get her grade easily enough if she wanted to. The thing is to study hard. She's getting to be a big girl now and should realize that. What is the capital of Canada, Victoria?"
> Jane knew perfectly well what the capital of Canada was but Uncle William fired the question at her so unexpectedly and all the guests stopped eating to listen . . . and for the moment she couldn't remember for her life what the name was. She blushed . . . stammered . . . squirmed. If she had looked at mother she would have seen that mother was forming the word silently on

her lips, but she could not look at any one. She was ready to die of shame and mortification.

"Phyllis," said Uncle William, "tell Victoria what the capital of Canada is."

Phyllis promptly responded.

"Ottawa."

"O-t-t-a-w-a," said Uncle William to Jane.

. . . Jane dropped her fork and writhed in anguish when she caught grandmother's eye. Grandmother touched her little silver bell.

"Will you bring Miss Victoria *another* fork, Davis," she said in a tone implying that Jane had had several forks already.

Every child has sat at that dinner table and not known the right answer. Every child has dropped her fork when all she had left was her dignity. Every child has not been Emily or Anne for they were children with something special about them. We all hope we possess that magic extra ingredient that sees Emily and Anne through, but underneath that hope lies the hard knowledge that we are fork-droppers.

The happy ending to *Jane of Lantern Hill* when the butterfly mother and the perfect father are reunited was not the part I reread and teasured most. I lingered over and loved Jane's times of personal triumph. When Cousin Phyllis, she who was so ready with the capital of Canada, comes to the Island on vacation with her family, she spends a day with Jane. First Jane cooks well. Phyllis gasps. Then Jane swims capably. Phyllis, once more, is suitably impressed. (Notice that Jane does NOT read Phyllis a poem which is wonderful beyond anything Phyllis or I could ever produce. Jane does things anybody who cared enough could learn to do.) Then the two girls set out to walk Phyllis back to her hotel. Phyllis is afraid of the dark; Phyllis falls climbing over a fence; Phyllis is reduced to quivering terror at the sight of some cows. That Jane has had to conquer some trepidation over cows herself, a while before, lends a beautifully realistic touch.

"Oh, what's that?" Phyllis clutched Jane.
"That? Only cows.'
"Oh, Victoria, I'm so scared of them. I can't pass them. I can't . . . Suppose they think . . . "
"Who cares what a cow thinks?" said Jane superbly.

Who cares what a cow thinks? Who cares what the capital of Canada is, Phyllis? Not Jane. Never again. Phyllis, to the reader's intense pleasure, sobs pitifully,

"Will you . . . walk between me . . . and the cows?"

Jane consents. She is comforting, protective, kindness itself -- and very humanly delighted with her own performance.

Did Montgomery, in writing this last book, deliberately turn away from writing about the special children who had made her famous? Was she looking for more reality?

I doubt that she was consciously doing so for the reality is always there even when it is less easy to find than in *Jane of Lantern Hill*. The burning embarrassment of having to wear the wrong clothes to school, the shock of betrayal when your "best friend" turns out to be a snake in the grass, the desolation of homesickness, the impossibility of communicating the urgency of childhood to adults who never doubt that tomorrow will be soon enough, the naming of special places with private names, the fear of Judgement Day and of cows, all of these and so much more Lucy Maud Montgomery records faithfully and with complete identification. So children will continue to find themselves in her pages. They will have to skip because there is a lot of waste space there too, but rage, wonder, laughter, misery, resentment, panic, ecstasy, failure, love, and insight wait therein between the inconsequential parts. And the dreams are there! Because if Anne, who was taken in by mistake, if Emily, who was given a home by the drawing of lots, and if Jane, who did not know the capital of Canada, can all make it through to victory, maybe we can too.

Is it Canadian Children's Literature though?

. . . In a recent letter to Rosemary Sutcliff, I mentioned getting ready to write this article. One paragraph in her reply answers that question so much better than I can that I will let her, the writer she is now and the child, albeit English, she so clearly remembers being, finish for me:

> . . . About the L. M. Montgomery books, this Emily you mention
> among her heroines, isn't by *any* chance, *Emily of New Moon* is
> she? Because I read that in hospital, aged about twelve, -- sleeping
> out-of-doors in part of the Ward, and reading in the summer dusk
> with the stars pricking out, and the bugles from the distant
> barracks sounding 'Lights Out'. And it remains magic in my mind,
> and I have never been able to trace it because of not knowing
> who it was by. If it *is* one of hers, it's probably one of the
> bad ones but, oh, how I loved it!

NOTES

[1] Lucy Maud Montgomery, *The Alpine Path* (Toronto: Fitzhenry & Whiteside, 1917), p. 78.

[2] *Ibid.*, p. 16.

[3] Helen M. Ridley, *The Story of L. M. Montgomery* 1874-1942 (Toronto: McGraw-Hill Ryerson, 1956), p. 130.

Jean Little is the internationally translated author of many children's novels -- Mine for Keeps, One to Grow On, From Anna, Kate, *and others* -- *and winner of the Little, Brown Canadian Children's Book Award. Her most recent book is* Stand in the Wind, *published this Autumn.*